RULES

Gene Buckelew

Rules Copyright @ 2023 by Gene Buckelew

Requests for information should be sent via email to rulesgenebuckelew@gmail.com

Scripture quotations marked ESV are taken from the ESV® Bible (The Holy Bible, English Standard Version®). Copyright © 2001 by Crossway, a publishing ministry of Good News Publishers. Used by permission. All rights reserved.

All rights reserved. No part of this book, including icons and images, may be reproduced in any manner without prior written permission from the copyright holder, except where noted in the text and in the case of brief quotations in critical articles and reviews.

All emphases in Scripture quotations are the author's.

I want to thank my wife, Tracy, for believing I could accomplish this work. Over the years, she has been my friend, my love, my encouragement, and my life.

Cover design: Steven Novak

Special Acknowledgments:
Sarah Michelle
Aubrey Ukuku
Lou Ann Franke
Kelsey Gallant
Tracy Buckelew

Contents

Introduction 7

1. Rule of Definition 23
Define the term or words being considered and then adhere to the defined meanings.

2. Rule of Usage 31
Words have meaning, and the usage of words produces concepts.

3. Rule of Context 49
Context must define terms and how words are used.

4. Rule of Historical Insight 57
Don't separate interpretation and historical investigation.

5. Rule of Relevance 71
Have a bearing on or connection with the matter at hand. Have a purposeful meaning and application in the life of the hearers or readers.

6. Rule of Precedents 79
Use the known and commonly accepted meanings of words, not obscure meanings for which there is no precedent.

7\. RULE OF UNITY 85
Even though many documents may be used, there must be a general unity among them.

8\. RULE OF INFERENCE 93
Base conclusions on what is already known, proven, or can be reasonably inferred from all known facts.

9\. RULE OF LOGIC 97
Be certain that words as interpreted agree with the overall premise.

10\. THE SCHEME OF REDEMPTION 105
The "Scheme of Redemption" explains the whole Bible narrative.

11\. THE COVENANT 113
Explaining what a covenant is and how God uses them.

Invitation to Contribute 127

Epilogue 129

About the Author 133

Introduction

Have you ever thought about Scripture as evidence of how much God loves us and wants us to know him and his ways? He is invested in us. God has always cared for man. He created a garden for Adam and Eve. He walked with the Patriarchs. He saved the Israelites from slavery and gave them a leader in Moses who brought them closer to God. He gave them the Law and taught them to be different than the nations around them. He sent his son as a sacrifice for our sin. Jesus, on the night he was betrayed, promised us a new covenant and a new kind of relationship with God. Look at Paul's letter to the Corinthians:

"Therefore, if anyone is in Christ, he is a new creation. The old has passed away; behold, the new has come. All this is from God . . ." (2 Cor. 5:17–18).

We see the Father's dedication to us through the words he imparts in the Scriptures. Through his Word, God reveals his previously hidden wisdom. Consider Paul's words to the church in Ephesus:

> Of this gospel I was made a minister according to the gift of God's grace, which was given me by the working of his power. To me, though I am the very least of all the

> saints, this grace was given, to preach to the Gentiles the unsearchable riches of Christ, and to bring to light for everyone what is the plan of the mystery hidden for ages in God, who created all things, so that through the church the manifold wisdom of God might now be made known to the rulers and authorities in the heavenly places. This was according to the eternal purpose that he has realized in Christ Jesus our Lord, in whom we have boldness and access with confidence through our faith in him. (Eph. 3:7–12)

Paul says that without the Spirit's words revealing the deep things of God and Christ, we would know nothing of his character. Yes, creation shows us there is a God. But we can perceive his wisdom only through his words to us—the words and truth that God knew we needed in order to faithfully trust and follow him. As Christians, we have a different lens through which to view life, people, and God's Word. God tells us that all Scripture is from him. We couldn't possibly know his plan to create, rescue, redeem, and restore us if the Spirit hadn't revealed this in his words. We wouldn't even know there was a problem God had to address. So words have meaning, and it is in this meaning that we find life. Peter explains to us that God is the only purveyor of revelation:

> We ourselves heard this very voice borne from heaven. . . . And we have the prophetic word more fully confirmed, to which you would do well to pay attention . . . knowing this first of all, that no prophecy of Scripture comes from someone's own interpretation. For no prophecy was ever

produced by the will of man, but men spoke from God as they were carried along by the Holy Spirit. (2 Pet. 1:18–21)

When Peter says, "You will do well to pay attention," he means they should understand something. But how can they pay attention to this something if they all see something differently? Peter is not asking them to do the impossible. Peter is assuming all of the hearers know exactly what to do. He expects everyone to interpret his words collectively. The relevance of the Scripture to their lives depends on it. Peter expects them to all use the same rules of interpretation to understand what he says.

Interpreting the Bible

When we first start studying the Scriptures, we begin as students with little experience in handling the Word. Gradually, we study and learn with teachers and mentors by our side, repeating what we learned from them. But at some point, God expects us to grow in our understanding of his Word and apply Scripture to our lives—making the Bible personal to us. At some point in studying God's Word for ourselves, we may gain a clearer and deeper understanding . . . we become more experienced.

Paul told Timothy to be careful with how he teaches the Word. If Paul warned Timothy to "handle the word correctly," that means there is a *wrong* way to handle it, and Timothy would have to understand the difference. The only way Timothy could accomplish this was if he had a set of rules to guide him. The reason my book is called *Rules* is that I believe Timothy followed these rules I am presenting to you and that is how he knew how to handle the Word correctly.

The Relevance of Scripture

First-century Christians studied the Old Testament and tried to understand the promises spoken by God's messengers. Through the apostles, the early church had the advantage of fifteen hundred years of Old Testament history revealed directly to them. This is something we do not have today. What we do have in the New Testament is the explanation of what God accomplished in those people.

Contrary to what some people may believe, the Scriptures were not written to us directly. When we assume we're the intended audience, we misrepresent the intent of the authors. In the first century, those who followed Jesus had to wrestle with the Old Testament. But they had inspired leaders—the apostles—to make it relevant to them.

Now, over two thousand years removed, we must wrestle in a different way to make the Scriptures relevant to us. We must study to pull out the meaning so that we can apply these teachings.

The Word was written in the past, and we must view it as history. Scripture wasn't written to speculate on what will happen, but rather to help us understand what God has done in history, his history of dealing with man's predicament. We were made without sin. When we were born, we were sinless. But at some point, we sinned and fell short of the glorious God. God would like to make us spiritually mature, full of wisdom and stable in all our ways. It's why we are drawn to the Bible. It's the way the words appeal to us. We know there is something missing. God communicates to our needs with words. Although the words weren't written to us, they have meaning to us. The Bible may be history, but the words transcend history. They are relevant to our special needs.

Introduction

Think about it. We do not have the partial Word of God. We have the complete, God-breathed Word delivered by the Holy Spirit. We don't have the apostles or other inspired followers to tell us what their words meant as they presented them for the first time, working miracles to back up their words, because that's not necessary now. Nothing can be added—nothing new has been written by the Holy Spirit since the first century.

We want to know what the Bible means for us, but we simply cannot make it mean anything that pleases us and makes us feel good about ourselves and then give the Holy Spirit "credit."

The bottom line is that the Holy Spirit cannot be used to contradict Scripture because all Scripture is inspired by the Spirit, and the Spirit inspired the authors' original intent. Scripture didn't come by the hand of man but by the hand of God. It was completely delivered by the Holy Spirit:

> All Scripture is God-breathed and is useful for instruction, for conviction, for correction, and for training in righteousness, so that the man of God may be complete, fully equipped for every good work. (2 Tim. 3:16–17)

Paul writes of things that are not known apart from the Spirit of God:

> See to it that no one takes you captive by philosophy and empty deceit, according to human tradition, according to the elemental spirits of the world, and not according to Christ. For in him the whole fullness of deity dwells bodily, and you have been filled in him, who is the head of all rule and authority. (Col. 2:8–10)

And again, Paul writes of the worthlessness of man's wisdom:

> And my speech and my message were not in plausible words of wisdom, but in demonstration of the Spirit and of power, so that your faith might not rest in the wisdom of men but in the power of God. Yet among the mature we do impart wisdom, although it is not the wisdom of this age or of the rulers of this age, who are doomed to pass away. But we impart a secret and hidden wisdom of God, which God decreed before the ages for our glory. None of the rulers of this age understood this, for if they had, they would not have crucified the Lord of glory. But, as it is written, "What no eye has seen, nor ear heard, nor the heart of man imagined, what God has prepared for those who love him"—these things God has revealed to us through the Spirit. For the Spirit searches everything, even the depths of God. For who knows a person's thoughts except the spirit of that person, which is in him? So also no one comprehends the thoughts of God except the Spirit of God. Now we have received not the spirit of the world, but the Spirit who is from God, that we might understand the things freely given us by God. And we impart this in words not taught by human wisdom but taught by the Spirit, interpreting spiritual truths to those who are spiritual. The natural person does not accept the things of the Spirit of God, for they are folly to him, and he is not able to understand them because they are spiritually discerned. The spiritual person judges all things but is himself to be judged by no one. "For who has understood the mind of the Lord so as to instruct him?" But we have the mind of Christ. (1 Cor. 2:4–16)

Introduction

The Spirit's help for us comes through our own discovery of the authors' original intent and as the Spirit guides us when we faithfully work to apply the Word to our lives.

I know firsthand that discovery and application are by no means easy to do, but as Scripture tells us, those who abide in him and write the Word on their hearts will be considered faithful. If it were easy, Jesus would never have said: "Blessed are those who hunger and thirst for righteousness, for they will be filled" (Matt. 5:6).

In the first century, the writer of the book of Hebrews tells the Jews: "In the past, God spoke to our ancestors through the prophets at many times and in various ways, but in these last days he has spoken to us by his Son, whom he appointed heir of all things, and through whom also he made the universe" (Heb. 1:1).

Peter writes about the knowledge we need to live righteously. Look at his words: "His divine power has given us everything we need for a godly life through our knowledge of him who called us by his own glory and goodness" (2 Pet. 1:3).

By "knowledge of him" we grow in faith (Rom. 10:17). Knowledge comes from studying his words. It takes study to understand the Word of God. We can't leave out the Holy Spirit, and we can't leave ourselves out of the equation. The Lord requires fertile soil to produce a harvest in us. Our hearts need to be tuned to the words of the Spirit. Consider Jesus' parable of the sower in Mark's Gospel: "Still other seed fell on good soil, where it sprouted, grew up, and produced a crop" (Mark 4:8).

The seed is the Word, and the soil is our hearts.

Faith equals trust. If we don't see faith as a tangible product of God's Word (hearing, believing, and trusting), then we assume that faith is an experiential magic formula that saves us. With those assumptions, our practice will be confined to what produces a feeling of false security in us. *For faith comes from hearing and hearing by the Word of God.* So there is a basis by which faith is proven and a plan by which it grows in us. It's trust in God and his plan.

Preparing to Read the Bible

In reading the Bible, carefully read the author's introduction and his statement of purpose. The introduction puts the letter in the context of history. In other words, the introduction states its relevance and application to the intended audience. It also identifies the author and the subject matter. Note the author's reason for writing. Nothing is written without a purpose.

As we study, it's our job to identify the author's reason for writing. Also, his audience is a major part of understanding the intent and whether his writing has a practical application to us today. Or is it bound to that culture or particular time? That is, was the intent for a period of time, or should it be continued in the present day?

Sometimes the author's intent is to address a problem or multiple problems in the church. After addressing the problem, the author usually gives a solution. Typically it is God's solution, although at times it is the author's opinion. Paul clearly writes: "In my judgment, she is happier if she stays as she is—and I think that I too have the Spirit of God" (1 Cor. 7:40). Here, the apostle clearly states that his words are his opinion. We may have to take into consideration the circumstances his advice is referring to. When Paul is writing these words the church was being persecuted. It was a difficult time which may have been complicated by a life choice, even if it were acceptable to God.

Introduction

Always be aware of corroborating thought. A good example is that Solomon's thoughts are very similar to Paul's statement to Timothy that all Scripture is profitable for teaching and training (2 Tim. 3:16).

> The proverbs of Solomon son of David, king of Israel:
> for gaining wisdom and instruction;
> for understanding words of insight;
> for receiving instruction in prudent behavior,
> doing what is right and just and fair;
> for giving prudence to those who are simple, a
> knowledge and discretion to the young—
> let the wise listen and add to their learning,
> and let the discerning get guidance—
> for understanding proverbs and parables,
> the sayings and riddles of the wise.
> The fear of the Lord is the beginning of knowledge,
> but fools despise wisdom and instruction. (Prov. 1:1–7)

I should note here that a "proverb" is a general truth, good advice, and wise practice. Proverbs always depend on one's ability to follow them to a greater or lesser degree, not what we would call an absolute, as some might believe. "Train up a child in the way he should go, and when he is old he will not depart from it" is a general truth. It depends on the child's ability to practice what he has been taught. It also depends on how well the parent diminishes their character flaws—what Exodus calls sin. A general statement of the word "sin" is not clearly understood by the reader. Therefore, what a father actually practices that a child would accept as normal is a character flaw. It would be continual sinning in which a child would be trained. Thus, a character flaw, such as lying, would affect a child.

Look at the overall message of a book.

In John's Gospel, he states that his reason for writing is to witness to the deity of Jesus in creation—that he is everlasting. Read and let this sink in:

> In the beginning was the Word, and the Word was with God, and the Word was God. He was with God in the beginning. Through him all things were made; without him nothing was made that has been made. In him was life, and that life was the light of all mankind. The light shines in the darkness, and the darkness has not overcome it. (John 1:1–5)

At the end of John, the disciple shares the reason for his bold witness:

> This is the disciple who testifies to these things and who wrote them down. We know that his testimony is true. Jesus did many other things as well. If every one of them were written down, I suppose that even the whole world would not have room for the books that would be written. (John 21:24)

You can see that everything between these passages relates to these two statements.

A good way to identify intent is to ask these questions:

- Who: Who is the audience?
- What: What is the subject?
- When: What is the timeframe in history?

- Where: Where did it occur?
- Why: What was the problem the author was trying to convey?
- How: How do they/we resolve the problem?

Also look at these three areas:

- Observation: Why did the writer bother to write?
- Situations: What was the author addressing that he expected his audience to respond to?
- Possible application: Were there any actions the author required?

Why We Need the Rules

We can't know the clear intent of Scripture if we don't have rules to help us. All false doctrine and error come from violating one or more of the rules I write about in this book—rules that neither Jesus nor his apostles violated in their teaching and letters.

The Old Testament's specific purpose is to point to the Messiah and his redemptive work in restoring man to his previous spiritual relationship with God. The specific purpose of the New Testament is to take that "restored" relationship to the rest of the world. When we miss those purposes, we misunderstand and maybe even miss the promises.

I fully believe that God created these "Rules of Interpretation" when he created language. Yes, I said when "HE" created language. If we violate the rules that God uses or the Bible writers used to communicate to us, we could dream up almost anything and believe it to be true. False teachers could tell us anything that remotely sounds right to us, and we could follow it to our detriment. We read the Bible with good intentions but never really grow our faith. We never clearly see the written purpose or God's inspiration for the authors' words. However, if we have rules for interpreting the Bible, we will see a sharp contrast between what some say and what WE see in Scripture.

Here is what the writer of the book of Hebrews has to say to that:

> For though by this time you ought to be teachers, you need someone to teach you again the basic principles of the oracles of God. You need milk, not solid food, for everyone who lives on milk is unskilled in the word of righteousness, since he is a child. But solid food is for the mature, for those who have their powers of discernment trained by constant practice to distinguish good from evil. (Heb. 5:12–14)

To help us understand his Word, God put forth rules. He created the way we communicate truths. He gave us a pattern to follow while interpreting what the Holy Spirit delivered: "Hold on to the pattern of sound teaching you have heard from me" (2 Tim. 1:13).

Let's think about the nature of patterns: A pattern demands structure. A pattern demands that things fit together only one way. It can be reproduced over and over again and yields the same results every single time with no variations. This pattern of "holding on to sound teaching" that Paul writes about shows itself in the rules that God created for all literature. Otherwise, there is no understanding whatsoever. Without these rules, we can't understand any historical document, the plot of a novel, or the Bible. Everything hinges on these rules being handled correctly. Without the way God made language to function, words become meaningless mounds of gibberish, and sentences become meaningless.

If we misunderstand this pattern that God has set forth, our inability—not God's negligence—is at fault.

If Scripture could be interpreted by our feelings and not by rules, no one would be able to agree on anything. That is the problem we must face. It may sound harsh, but it's true. Without rules, we are merely "pooling our ignorance."

God expects us to understand the words he has given us—the truths he imparts to us. And if our Lord expects us to understand what he imparts, then he has surely given us the tools we need to interpret those truths.

The rules I've studied and write about in this book are the center of all grammatical interpretation. They were realized and developed by specialists in the "science of meaning" over the past 2,500 years. From Socrates to the present day, these rules apply equally to legislative or theological language. Without them, critical analysis is impossible. Interpretive scholarship accepts them. And we, as God's church and his bride, can surely benefit from them as we press into this invaluable gift our Father has given us in his Word.

> A wise man will hear, and will increase learning . . . to understand a proverb, and the interpretation.
>
> —Solomon in Proverbs 1:5–6

> Be diligent to present yourself approved to God, a worker who does not need to be ashamed, rightly dividing (handling well) the word of truth.
>
> —the apostle Paul in 2 Timothy 2:15

My entire book is a way of summarizing the rules of interpretation so that you can see them together in one place. It is not intended to be an exhaustive attempt to present these rules and their application but an overview for your consideration:

1. Rule of Definition

Define the term or words being considered and then adhere to the defined meanings.

2. Rule of Usage

Words have meaning, and the usage of words produces concepts.

3. Rule of Context

Context must define terms and how words are used.

4. Rule of Historical Insight

Don't separate interpretation and historical investigation.

5. Rule of Relevance

Have a bearing on or connection with the matter at hand. Have a purposeful meaning and application in the life of the hearers or readers.

6. Rule of Precedent

Use the known and commonly accepted meanings of words, not obscure meanings for which there is no precedent.

7. Rule of Unity

Even though many documents may be used, there must be a general unity among them.

8. Rule of Inference

Base conclusions on what is already known, proven, or can be reasonably inferred from all known facts.

9. Rule of Logic

Be certain that words as interpreted agree with the overall premise.

10. The Scheme of Redemption

The "Scheme of Redemption" explains the whole Bible narrative.

11. The Covenant

Explaining what a covenant is and how God uses them.

CHAPTER 1

The Rule of Definition

Define your terms and then keep to the terms defined.

"Any study of Scripture . . . must begin with a study of words."
— Theologian and apologist Bernard Ramm

When I first started out trying to make sense of what I read while studying the Bible, I was confused. As with most students, I was told to look words up in a Bible dictionary. I thought to myself, "How is any beginning student or the average person sitting in church going to understand for themselves word definitions?" They didn't know the Greek language that preachers and teachers referred to. I didn't know the Greek language back then. Why aren't we teaching people how to study the Bible for themselves? It seemed to me if, as my professors always said, "The Bible is its own best dictionary," then we should be teaching students to go to the Bible first instead of the dictionary. Enter the Rule of Definition.

Defining terms is essential to understanding Scripture. The definition of a word must make sense and complement its context. The Bible is an excellent dictionary in and of itself. We want the Scriptures to explain definitions and word usage for us because a modern-day dictionary cannot contextually and accurately explain and interpret ancient Bible terms. Analysis of words can be done only in their context.

> DEFINING TERMS IS ESSENTIAL TO UNDERSTANDING SCRIPTURE.

The writers of the Bible could not coin new words because they would not be understood, so they used the words already in use in their day.

Consider that a word is never used outside of (1) a sentence with specific information delivered by the author, (2) a paragraph presenting a logical progression of thought, or (3) a collection of paragraphs in which the author presents a complete explanation, narrative, or argument.

Words are the basic building block for conveying meaning. In exegesis, it is especially important to remember that words function in a context. Although a given word may have a broad or narrow range of meaning, the aim of word study is to try to understand as precisely as possible what the author was meaning to convey by their use of the word in this context. Thus, for example, you cannot legitimately do a word study of "flesh"; you can only do a word study of "flesh" in 1 Corinthians 5:5 or 2 Corinthians 5:16, and so on.

Let's look at some specific word studies.

Word Studies

Sin

In Romans, Paul helps us define the word "sin" by explaining the result of sin: "For all have sinned and fall short of the glory of God" (Rom. 3:23).

To fall short is to miss the mark. We could say to miss the mark is to miss a target, to indicate that the arrow didn't hit the bull's-eye. It fell short. So the definition of sin is to fail to live up to God's intent for our lives. We fall short of his excellence. That is the simple definition of sin.

Parable

Let's look at the word "parable" in a different way. We don't use the word "parable" in modern-day life, but it is easy to see that it is a simple story to provide a more profound meaning. Parables are used to teach an underlying message. The intent here is to try to define words by looking at word usage or clear explanations in Scripture. That is the way most of us will have to define words if we don't have the knowledge of the original languages of the Bible. Jesus used parables in a way that would define the word for us. We can see that Jesus told stories with spiritual meanings. So we know that Jesus' purpose for the parables he told was to impart a message. Jesus himself said that some would understand the meaning, and some would not. He emphasized that their understanding would depend on the condition of their heart:

> The disciples came to him and asked, "Why do you speak in parables?" He replied, "Because the knowledge of the secrets of the kingdom of heaven has been given to

> you, but not to them . . . This is why I speak to them in parables." (Matt. 13:10–11, 13)

Jesus' explanation didn't mean that some people are chosen to be saved or elected, as some think, but that their heart would set their destiny unless their heart changed.

> Other seeds fell on good soil and produced grain, some a hundredfold. . . . As for what was sown on good soil, this is the one who hears the word and understands it. He indeed bears fruit . . . ." (Matt. 13:8, 23)

Jesus said that some would not understand the message in the parable because they weren't seeking God. They may have believed they had already arrived spiritually, as in the case of the self-righteous leaders who would later reject the Messiah, their promised Savior. So we can see that a parable was a simple story that told a spiritual truth that those with willing hearts would understand but those with hard hearts wouldn't.

But we shouldn't always define a word in the Bible using only one passage. To get a clear picture of a particular word's definition, we need to study how it is used in multiple references. It is the same for a biblical concept or phrase.

Isaiah gives us insight into the reason for parables, thus reinforcing the definition of the word: "Go, and say to this people: 'Keep on hearing, but do not understand; keep on seeing, but do not perceive,' (Isa. 6:9).

The people heard the story, and most generally did not understand the purpose because there was a message "cast alongside" the story—what we would now call an "underlying message."

Jesus told parables when the religious leaders came to test him. In the parables, he gave them an answer to their questions, but because of the condition of their hearts, they didn't understand what he was telling them.

> You will be ever hearing but never understanding; you will be ever seeing but never perceiving. For this people's heart has become calloused; they hardly hear with their ears, and they have closed their eyes. Otherwise they might see with their eyes, hear with their ears, understand with their hearts and turn, and I would heal them. (Matt. 13:14–15)

So we can see that a parable is a story with an underlying message that a person with a fertile heart could understand but those with hardened hearts could not.

NATION/NATIONS

The word "nation" or its plural is usually mistranslated because many see it as an extension of the United Nations. When we think of nations, we see a picture of the whole globe and the nations of the world. "Nation" couldn't have meant anything close to that to the ancients, such as Abraham. They had no visual of an earth as we know it. We need to be careful not to define words in the Bible with our modern knowledge and experience. For the people of the Old Testament, "nation" was more closely attuned to earth as in soil, farm, or land. Look at God's words to Abraham in Genesis: "Abraham will surely become a great and powerful nation" (Gen. 18:18).

It would make more sense for Abraham to think of "land" when he heard this because what he visualized was the land that God promised him and his offspring—what we would know as the children of Abraham who inherited the Promised Land, or his descendants who lived on the land.

So in biblical times, "nation" would have meant the land where people live, whether it was where Abraham came from or where he was promised he was going.

It is true that the world got bigger as we progressed through Scripture, but we have to be content with the characters' view during their time period. Even in Paul's time he referred to the world he knew and not the world we know. We know the world was bigger than Paul knew, but that doesn't seem to be what Jesus had in mind based on what he said before his death, in Mark 16:15: "Go into all the world and proclaim the Gospel to the whole creation."

We can be sure the gospel went as far Rome, because Paul said so. What we can't be sure of is that it went to India or beyond. No New Testament writer ever speaks about that. So, when Paul refers to "all creation under heaven," we have to be satisfied with what Paul understood to be the then-known world.

Miracles

We often hear someone say about a severely sick loved one unexpectedly recovering that it was a miracle. I'll accept that as a modern-day definition, but what does the Bible say was a true biblical miracle? What are we really after when we study the Bible? We are after facts first, and then the practical application of those facts as they should fit into our lives.

One passage that gives us some insight on miracles is in Luke 22:50–51: "One of them struck the servant of the high priest and cut off his right ear. But Jesus said, 'No more of this!' And he touched his ear and healed him." There is a big difference between a man having his ear restored by touch and having a surgeon stitch it back on. My point here is that Jesus went outside the realm of our physical universe to accomplish this. A

Chapter 1 · The Rule of Definition

surgeon works within the limits of the physical world to accomplish his task.

Another fact about biblical miracles is that they all have verifiable witnesses.

Miracles are supernatural by their nature, and they were always witnessed by others. However, there is one other element of a biblical miracle: its deniability. The book of Acts contains many miracles performed by Peter, Paul, and others. In one example in Acts, Peter was called before the rulers, elders, Annas the high priest, Caiaphas, John, Alexander, and all who were of the high priest's family. That's a lot of witnesses. Peter had healed a lame man and was called before these men to give an account of his actions. These rulers quizzed Peter, saying, "By what power or by what name did you do this?" (Acts 4:7). Already they are admitting that the miracle of healing the lame man went outside of earthly authority, meaning it was supernatural.

Reading further in this context we'll notice the three elements that make up a biblical definition of a miracle.

> Seeing the man who was healed standing beside them (Peter and John), they (the counsel) had nothing to say in opposition . . . they (the counsel) conferred with one another, saying, "What shall we do with these men? For that a notable sign has been performed through them is evident to all the inhabitants of Jerusalem, and we cannot deny it." (Acts 4:14–4:16)

So the definition of a true biblical miracle is that it is supernatural, witnessed by all who were there (the witnesses all saw the same thing), and can't be denied.

CHAPTER 2

THE RULE OF USAGE

Words have meaning, and how they're used produces concepts.

Analysis of words can be done only in their context of usage. Understanding human language and how it is formed to communicate purpose is the key to understanding intent and seeing concepts or ideas. Sometimes we say that if we had all the particulars of a situation or event, we could see the "bigger picture."

Jesus was the master of giving his audience the bigger picture. The content and particulars of Jesus' words produce faith, and faith produces hope. And hope is the end result of understanding the words of Jesus. Hope is the thing humanity most desires. For without hope, we live in despair. There is nothing left.

Jesus came to give us hope, and he did this through the usage of words. Words make up language, and with the use of words, Jesus unveiled the mysteries of God: the vision of an unseen world.

Jesus' words give us true purpose and faith; the assurance of things hoped for. With the words he uses, he gives us something beyond this mere existence:

"So faith comes from hearing, and hearing through the word of Christ" (Rom. 10:17).

"Now faith is the assurance of things hoped for, the conviction of things not seen" (Heb. 11:1).

When God created individuals in his own likeness, he fashioned them with the ability to communicate and, with that, develop relationships. Animals don't possess the ability to communicate with language; it's uniquely human.

The use of language gives us communication, enabling us to understand what another person is thinking or feeling. In turn, communication facilitates meaningful relationships, which connect us with love and friendship—an absolute requirement of healthy human life. Communication depends on both the sender and the receiver of the communication, which depends on the sender's accuracy with using words to communicate their thoughts—and how accurately the receiver understands the sender's words.

In the case of Scripture, God is the sender through human "transmission." We are the receptors, and our task is to make sure we understand the author's intended meaning. Another way to explain this is that the Holy Spirit authored the Bible, using human messengers to write it down.

Interestingly enough, there is a reason the Holy Spirit used individuals throughout the ages to communicate his words. Their ability to write during the shifting cultural norms was imperative. They would understand their culture, language,

Chapter 2 · The Rule of Usage

definitions of colloquial words, and word usage. So they would write the Spirit's words with the ability to communicate each unique book, letter, or prophetic writing within the reader's understanding—especially with prophetic material, which takes a great deal of metaphorical and idiomatic word usage tied to the reader's ability to understand.

The readers are always the interpreters. The interpreters must try to understand what the Holy Spirit intended for them to perceive. The Holy Spirit uses what readers can understand, and that produces comprehension. This is where we get the unity of the whole narrative of the Bible. It fits together perfectly without any confusion. If we are confused, then we as the receptors are mistaken. When we approach the Scriptures, we should come in humility, acknowledging that we don't know everything. No one does, and we should be careful if our teachers never admit that. Responses like "I don't know, but I will study that and get back to you" or "Let's look at that together" reflect a humble and teachable heart. We can't all be teachers, and teachers need to be students too.

> THE HOLY SPIRIT USES WHAT READERS CAN UNDERSTAND, AND THAT PRODUCES COMPREHENSION.

Interpreting the Bible is no different than interpreting any other writing, letter, or document. They all require rules of language. Without those rules and an understanding of how language is used, we won't be able to accurately understand what God wants to reveal to us—and what he wants from us and for us. The interesting fact is that nothing changes from language to language. Whether it's Greek, Hebrew, or English, the rules of interpretation are always the same.

If we don't know the rules, we won't be able to identify the truth when we hear so many confusing interpretations of the same Scripture. Confusion can rob people of their peace of mind and abundance of life—the hope that Jesus so often spoke about:

> But false prophets also arose among the people, just as there will be false teachers among you, who will secretly bring in destructive heresies. . . . And in their greed they will exploit you with false words. (2 Pet. 2:1, 3)

If we don't have a set of guidelines to test the Scriptures, we engage in a free-for-all. Anything goes because we aren't all on the same page. With this, our faith can be based on erratic notions—shifting sand.

> Everyone then who hears these words of mine and does them will be like a wise man who built his house on the rock. And the rain fell, and the floods came, and the winds blew and beat on that house, but it did not fall, because it had been founded on the rock. And everyone who hears these words of mine and does not do them will be like a foolish man who built his house on the sand. And the rain fell, and the floods came, and the winds blew and beat against that house, and it fell, and great was the fall of it. (Matt. 7:24–27)

How can we even attempt to understand and practice what Jesus is referring to here if there isn't a way to clearly understand how he uses words? The fact is, we can't practice what we don't understand. The old adage "You don't know what you don't know" will always apply.

The rules of interpreting language are accurate. So if a group of believers agrees on the rules of interpreting the Scriptures, they will be as close as possible to one another in knowledge, understanding, unity, and practice. If we are a unified people and there is a thing Jesus says is true, we should try to find it because not knowing it causes us to guess. Guessing causes division. There is no such thing as "my truth." If we accept the fact that "we don't know what we don't know," we can begin studying to find out what we don't know with humility.

Speaking of not being on the same page, consider the story of the Tower of Babel:

> And the LORD said, "If as one people speaking the same language they have begun to do this, then nothing they plan to do will be impossible for them. Come, let us go down and confuse their language so they will not understand each other." So the LORD scattered them from there over all the earth, and they stopped building the city." (Gen. 11:6–8)

The point is: if we can't communicate, we can't congregate. Speaking louder to a person who does not understand your language is absurd. Where fights and disagreements come from is being on different pages in defining our terms and how they're used.

If we aren't on the same page in this regard, we can't develop a unified, systematic, in-depth understanding of the Word of God. We are left with only what we feel is the truth. We build our house on the sand of feelings. Building our faith on feelings is backwards. But building our faith on truth gives us assurance. Faith is built on tangible words. With assurance that these words are true and understandable, we can have a basis whereby we can know our feelings are true.

Correctly understanding the meaning the author intended might be difficult since no two people have the same set of experiences and ideas. But through the rules of interpretation, we can create camaraderie of togetherness and understanding.

We can be on the same page.

As we see from the book of Hebrews, the Holy Spirit delivered the Bible's narrative to man. God spoke through many messengers. But the author was the Holy Spirit. The Holy Spirit used words to create the unity of purpose in the Scripture:

> Long ago, at many times and in many ways, God spoke to our fathers by the prophets, but in these last days he has spoken to us by his Son. (Heb. 1:1–2)

If we try to understand the words written down by the Holy Spirit—all having the same rules of interpretation—we can be united in that process, which will allow us to understand God's intended purpose. Those words will, in turn, give us patience and unity to love and help others become better adapted to opening the great riches of the Scriptures for themselves. They won't fall prey to the inconsistent use of God's Word.

However, in communicating with us, the Holy Spirit allowed for differences in culture, language, and writing style. In different ages and cultures, language looks different; interpretation is culturally different. We have to dig into how word usage in language and culture played a part in how the author communicated to his audience. For example, let's look at the phrase "a pig in a poke." A poke is a sack or bag, and to buy a pig in a poke is to purchase something sight unseen—something offered in such a way as to obscure its real nature or worth. In fourteenth-century jolly old England, the advice meant "don't buy anything until you have examined it."

One thing we should realize is that "God is not a God of confusion but of peace" (1 Cor. 14:33).

Because of this truth about God, the scriptures should be at peace with one another, not fight against one another. Also, we should understand that if we can find that the Scripture is at peace with itself, we will be at peace with one another.

A biblical author's words are precise, inspired of God. However, to us they may not seem so at face value. Words may not seem altogether precise, particularly when important abstract or figurative concepts are being communicated.

But that's not the author's fault; his reader/hearer is the problem. A person who would understand another must work on it. The person spoken to is always the interpreter; the speaker is always the author. It is true that the burden of communication is on the part of the author, but when you add in differing word usages throughout many different authors, and throughout four thousand years of revelation, therein lies the difficulty of the listener.

Determining usage includes determining who the original hearers were. We should always regard the Bible as written for "the Jew first." The Bible's words and idioms ought to be rendered according to Hebrew usage. Almost all the Bible is written to and for the Hebrew people. For the most part the Gentile world comes in after Jesus' resurrection.

From Acts to Revelation, we should exercise extra care as we read because the plot changes in the new covenant. Cultural elements, including Greek-speaking people groups, have been added to fulfill the promise to Abraham: "So that in Christ Jesus the blessing of Abraham might come to the Gentiles, so that we might receive the promised Spirit through faith" (Gal. 3:14).

However, keeping that promise ushered in a new level of difficulty in interpreting the Scriptures. Greek-speaking people groups of different cultures swallowed up by Alexander the Great were added. Paul's work as the apostle to the Gentiles ushered in a completely different set of problems for us as students. A new language, a new culture with new idioms and new ideologies, arrives, compounding the difficulty for us as interpreters.

Jesus lived under the Law and used words from the common understanding of his time. He did not speak in the tongues of angels, although he most certainly knew them. If he had, we could not have understood what he taught. He spoke plainly and simply so that his audience could understand his words. That is why his teachings are known as "the Word." Jesus develops faith in us through his words making sense to us, which we can follow with confidence. And that confidence of faith in him brings us hope.

"So faith comes from hearing, and hearing through the word of Christ" (Rom. 10:17).

"Now faith is the assurance of things hoped for, the conviction of things not seen" (Heb. 11:1).

We need to understand that throughout Jesus' whole ministry he spoke to the Jew and their word usages, not to the non-Jew. The Greek non-Jew was added to the mix later. What Paul says is true; faith does come through the words of Christ. However, Paul was adjusting Christ's words to the word usage of the non-Jew.

Separating the Old and New Testaments properly is also important in understanding word usage. We've been taught that the Gospels are in the New Testament. That is not true.

Chapter 2 · The Rule of Usage

Jesus lived under the Law that we do not practice. We don't sacrifice animals as the Law required. Just because people organized the books of the Bible in the way they did doesn't make it right. Simply by understanding word usage we can see that Jesus hadn't died yet so he couldn't have a New Testament, or as we commonly call it, a will. To have a will enforced, the testator has to die.

If we do not understand where we should separate the Testaments, we will drag some of the commands of the Old Testament into the New and confuse the usage of words. There are things that are useful to us from the Old Testament but are no longer commanded of us. For instance, the Sabbath as it is commanded under the Old Testament is useful to us but not *required* of us. Paul disqualifies the Sabbath in his letter to the Colossians:

> Therefore let no one pass judgment on you in questions of food and drink, or with regard to a festival or a new moon or a Sabbath. (Col. 2:16)

Using one example, Paul is broadly saying that no regulations and practices required of followers of God in the old covenant are required in the new covenant of Christ, for we are relieved of them. From this exercise we can see that the usage of the words in the Old Testament won't have the same usage and that we shouldn't automatically assume that the words from the Old Testament are applicable to us today.

> Now if the ministry of death, carved in letters on stone, came with such glory that the Israelites could not gaze at Moses' face because of its glory, which was being brought to an end, will not the ministry of the Spirit have even

> more glory? For if there was glory in the ministry of
> condemnation, the ministry of righteousness must far
> exceed it in glory. (2 Cor. 3:7–9)

The key to this passage is that Jesus is far better than the old Law. Though God made the old Law, he designed it for a purpose, which was coming to an end. It was only made for Israel and excluded the Gentiles. The fact is that we can only be under one covenant at a time. The old covenant had to end so the new could be established. Paul knew this, so in his usage of his words he makes this his main intent because in verse six he begins his argument with the statement: "Who has made us sufficient to be ministers of a new covenant" (2 Cor. 3:6). In 1 Corinthians Paul speaks of the men who seek glory and do not honor God. And by his references we can see that these men were teaching the constraints of the old Law that went away and not teaching freedom in the new covenant.

The letter of the Law could only condemn; and with what these men were teaching, if the Corinthian church accepted this teaching, it would put them in bondage to an old covenant that would cause a lot of disharmony with the member who didn't accept them. But Paul's message was that under the new covenant we have the mercy and righteousness of Christ.

We must discern and combine the difference in the usage of words that condemn and the usage of words that give life.

So it is not only important to understand word usage but also the intent of those words.

> Now before faith came, we were held captive under the
> law, imprisoned until the coming faith would be revealed.
> So then, the law was our guardian until Christ came, in

order that we might be justified by faith. But now that faith has come, we are no longer under a guardian, for in Christ Jesus you are all sons of God, through faith. (Gal. 3:23–26)

Was there faith under the Law? Sure there was. The usage of the word "faith" here refers to the new covenant that is the promise that faith connects us to Christ. Faith through knowledge and belief has always connected believers with God. He requires nothing less, even under the old Law.

"I desire steadfast love and not sacrifice, the knowledge of God rather than burnt offerings" (Hos. 6:6).

Getting word usage right will help us understand teaching and thus produce faith and hope.

Some teach that the Ten Commandments are required of us. There is some misunderstanding of the usage of words and the purpose of the old Law and why it was given to the Jews only, under Moses. In his letter to the church in Galatia, does Paul mean that we should not follow the Ten Commandments today? Not necessarily. Moral law was instituted in the beginning. Nine of the Ten Commandments are moral law. The Sabbath was added for a specific purpose. The Hebrews had just left Egypt where they were slaves. For them, there was no day of a beneficial rest.

There was also no clear vision of God's moral law that he wanted the Hebrews to return to. They weren't far off from being Egyptians. They were practically so. After all, they made a golden calf, a deity of Egypt. God needed to spell things out for them. He did this by commanding that they adhere to a set of commandments; nine of the commandments were rooted in creation, what I call "the natural order" which God wove into the fabric of morality. The one commandment that was not concerned with morality was to keep the Sabbath. It was a practical commandment. When indentured servitude was introduced in Israel, the Sabbath kept masters from working their brethren seven days a week. In Mark, we see Jesus correcting the leaders who erroneously made the Sabbath a burden.

"The Sabbath was made for man, not man for the Sabbath" (Mark 2:27).

So we see that the Sabbath was to benefit man and not burden him further. Jesus let them know that the Sabbath was a day of rest, not a day of regulations.

Does this mean that we are relieved from the commandment, "You shall not commit murder"? Nothing could be more absurd. In the new covenant, the moral code would be written on the heart and not on tablets of stone continually broken by the Israelites. Look at God's message to the Jews:

> Behold, the days are coming, declares the LORD, when I will make a new covenant with the house of Israel and the house of Judah, not like the covenant that I made with their fathers on the day when I took them by the hand to bring them out of the land of Egypt, my covenant that they broke, though I was their husband, declares the LORD. For this is the covenant that I will make with the house of Israel after those days, declares the LORD: I will put my law within them, and I will write it on their hearts. And I will be their God, and they shall be my people. And no longer shall each one teach his neighbor and each his brother, saying, "Know the LORD," for they shall all know me, from the least of them to the greatest, declares the LORD. I will

forgive their iniquity, and I will remember their sin no more. (Jer. 31:31–34)

Jesus' whole life was under the Law: "But when the fullness of time had come, God sent forth his Son, born of woman, born under the law" (Gal. 4:4).

Jesus was born and died under the Old Testament Law. He had to live perfectly under the old covenant Law to fulfill it and then remove it and replace it with the new covenant. You could say that God gave the old covenant Law to Israel so that they could see the difference between perfection and imperfection. Jesus is surely the shining example of that fact. The Jews couldn't live it, but one of their own could: the Messiah.

"For Christ is the end of the law for righteousness to everyone who believes" (Rom. 10:4).

This means that everything Jesus taught was under the authority of the Old Testament Law. It's where we get the declaration of "to the Jew first, then the Gentile (the non-Jew)."

Jesus' purpose was to redeem the Jew first and foremost; God promised Abraham he would be with him: "He answered, 'I was sent only to the lost sheep of the house of Israel'" (Matt. 15:24). So sometimes understanding word usage depends on searching for corroborating passages.

When we try to understand Jesus' word usage we must first apply it to a Jewish audience, his people. For example, if we believe the parables were written to us, we interpret them wrongly. They were presented in Jewish context so that the Jewish hearers would understand their meaning. They were spoken so they would be relevant to the Jew of the first century, not to us. If we think they were spoken to us, we will interpret them with our own ideas and idioms and will fail to properly apply the definitions and the usage of those words.

But although they weren't spoken directly to us, they were written down for our understanding, in the same manner as the Old Testament was written to the Jew: "For whatever was written in former days was written for our instruction, that through endurance and through the encouragement of the Scriptures we might have hope" (Rom. 15:4).

We have the Scriptures the Jews read, and we have the Scriptures they wrote. What a gift!

Christ spoke to the Jews of his day in their own Hebrew context, culture, and common vernacular. Even the words the Samaritan woman spoke were founded in Hebrew concepts. What she said applies to a collective Jewish belief, not to Jesus' as an individual: speaking to Jesus, she says, "But you say that in Jerusalem is the place where people ought to worship" (John 4:20). She had never met Jesus so she didn't get that idea from him.

Yet what Jesus says tells her that in the future, worship would be about the individual, not a collective people. Listen to his response:

> Jesus said to her, "Woman, believe me, the hour is coming when neither on this mountain nor in Jerusalem will you worship the Father. You worship what you do not know; we worship what we know, for salvation is from the Jews. But the hour is coming, and is now here, when the true worshipers will worship the Father in spirit and truth, for the Father is seeking such people to worship him. God is spirit, and those who worship him must worship in spirit and truth." (John 4:21–24)

Jesus' words—"salvation is from the Jews"—meant that God's whole purpose was that Christ, the Messiah, would come through Jewish lineage. And with that carried out, salvation could then be offered to the Gentiles. Look at Paul's words to the Jewish Christians of Galatia: "So that in Christ Jesus the blessing of Abraham might come to the Gentiles, so that we might receive the promised Spirit through faith" (Gal. 3:14).

So salvation came to us from a Jewish knowledge of God. If it were not for the Jew, we would have no knowledge of God whatsoever. The promise of the redeeming Messiah was a promise to the Jews first, but in the new kingdom it is offered to all.

Because Jesus spoke in her context and culture, the Samaritan woman understood the concepts he communicated. If she hadn't, she would not have been able to explain to others the intent of Jesus' words, and the gospel would not have spread as it did.

"Many Samaritans from that town believed in him because of the woman's testimony" (John 4:39).

The testimony she received from Jesus, using plain and simple words she could understand, was in her cultural understanding.

Jesus accepted the word usage he found existing during his earthly ministry. He did not alter it to something the people he spoke to wouldn't understand. We have to be careful not to alter his usage of words but to complement them.

Jesus of Nazareth was a Jew, and he spoke to and moved among Jews in Israel. He spoke first and directly to the Jews, and his words must have been intelligible to them. It is absolutely necessary to view his life and teaching with Jewish eyes. This creates the framework by which we understanding Jesus' word usage in his teaching.

The division of the Old and New Testament came after Jesus' death. Under the new covenant, Jesus' desire for us was ultimately to be his heirs. He, "the Testator," must die, as mentioned in the book of Hebrews, before a new "Testament" could come into effect: "For a will takes effect only at death, since it is not in force as long as the one who made it is alive" (Heb. 9:17).

This didn't happen until Jesus' death on the cross. We have a clearer picture of his will when we see Jesus, on the night he was betrayed, take the cup and say, "For this is my blood, which confirms the (new) covenant between God and his people. It is poured out as a sacrifice to forgive the sins of many" (Matt. 26:28).

Jesus' use of the word "covenant" here referred to his will, which would come to fruition upon his death and not until then. So at that point, as Paul says of the old covenant: "Now before faith came, we were held captive under the law, imprisoned until the coming of faith in Christ might be given to those who believe . . . we were held captive under the law . . . until Christ came" (Gal. 3:23–29).

He doesn't mean when Christ was born; he means after Christ did his redemptive work because it was prophesied that he should die to achieve his ultimate will, to usher in a new covenant: "This is my blood of the covenant, which is poured out for the forgiveness of sins" (Matt. 26:28).

When determining usage, we must strive to learn how the author used words or even Scripture quotations, not according to our word usage, but according to the writer's usage during his lifetime. Remember, the Bible wasn't written *to* us but it was written *for* us (for our understanding). So we see that word definitions are paramount, but how they're used can alter the way we handle a word. A word's usage, in its context and culture, must always be considered.

We need to know how words are being used to understand what we read. Defining a word is important, but understanding a word's usage both culturally and purposefully is critical.

CHAPTER 3

THE RULE OF CONTEXT

Every word read must be understood in the light of the words that come before and after it.

Scripture wasn't written to fit the chapter breaks we see in modern Bible translations. The division of chapters came much later. We must learn to look past those and determine where the author began their story or presentation, which would be complete arguments, stories, or explanations of previous revelation.

The words that surround words are as important as the initial definitions we talked about in Chapter 1 and the usage of words we talked about in Chapter 2. It isn't enough to initially define a word. Once defined, a word doesn't merely stand as a blockade against which everything else is measured; quite the contrary.

Maybe this progression of what we have examined so far will help:

Rule No. 1, the rule of definition, requires that we establish the definition of a word, and once it is defined, we must stay with that definition until usage and/or context forces us to accept an altered definition.

Rule No. 2, the rule of usage, is to understand the word's definition as it is used in context.

Rule No. 3, the rule of context, is to look at the word's definition and usage in the context of all of the information or arguments surrounding it.

This progression doesn't end with these three rules. It continues to build on itself throughout the rest of the rules of interpretation until we have the clearest perception of truth. Though in all of this we must remember that context—if not king of the rules—is surely a prince. The theory that we can just flip the Bible open, close our eyes, and point to a verse is just not logical. We need the critical factor of context. We can't possibly understand the narrative of the Bible outside the context in which it was written.

The whole Bible was written for one purpose: to tell the story of how God intended to solve the problem of man's fall through the coming of Christ. That is God's stated purpose in delivering the book.

The whole Bible tells us how, through a specific lineage, God brought that purpose to fruition through Christ. Everything that follows the fall is based on this first prophecy, which will inevitably be fulfilled by Jesus at the cross (*Satan's strike*) and the resurrection (*Jesus' crushing blow*).

Speaking to Satan, God said: "And I will put enmity between you and the woman, and between your seed and her seed. He will crush your head, and you will strike his heel" (Gen. 3:15).

The one who created the cosmos would be the one who chose to die on the cross for our sin, and in doing so he would crush Satan.

Having understood that, what we now attempt to do is return the narrative back to the specific context of the words, thoughts, and surroundings in which they were written.

The original manuscripts that make up the Bible were written without chapter and verse indicators. They seem to have been added without much thought to the context or, in some cases, logical progression of an argument. Although the numbers make it easier to find verses and words, they also may hinder our ability to identify context. So, when we study a passage in its context, we need to broaden our focus. We need to try to ignore the chapter and verse constraints and look fully at the progression of the author's thoughts on the subject at hand.

> **WHEN WE STUDY A PASSAGE IN ITS CONTEXT, WE NEED TO BROADEN OUR FOCUS.**

Examples of Context

The Strength Paul would receive from Christ.

"I can do all things through Christ who gives me strength" (Phil. 4:13).

Sometimes this verse is taken out of context and used as a motivator for people to win a race, climb a mountain, or build a business. When we widen our focus, we can see that is not the author's intent in its context.

> Now I rejoice greatly in the Lord that at last you have revived your concern for me. You were indeed concerned, but you had no opportunity to show it. I am not saying this out of need, for I have learned to be content regardless of my circumstances. I know how to live humbly, and I know how to abound. I am accustomed to any and every situation—to being filled and being hungry, to having plenty and having need. I can do all things through Christ who gives me strength. (Phil. 4:10–13)

When we read verses 10–13, we see Paul stating that through all of his suffering to advance his work, his strength comes from the fact that Christ suffered far worse than he has and that Christ is there beside him to encourage and help him in his time of suffering. Paul knows the sustainer of the universe is king over the seen and the unseen, and that God can, in fact, take care of him.

When we read Philippians 4:13 in context, we immediately see that the verse is not referring to winning or excelling in any earthly way, but rather to practicing contentment in how Christ looks over us, no matter how troublesome or hard our circumstances may be.

Let's broaden our study and see if we can learn more about Paul's letter to the Philippians.

> Nevertheless, you have done well to share in my affliction. And as you Philippians know, in the early days of the gospel, when I left Macedonia, no church but you partnered with me in the matter of giving and receiving. For even while I was in Thessalonica, you provided for my needs again and again. (Phil. 4:14–16)

The main subject Paul is commenting on here is the fact that the Philippians "partnered" with him by providing him with physical and monetary support so that he could continue his work. Indeed, this partnership was not only appreciated by Paul but by God also:

> Not that I am seeking a gift, but I am looking for the fruit that may be credited to your account. I have all I need and more, now that I have received your gifts from Epaphroditus. They are a fragrant offering, an acceptable sacrifice, well-pleasing to God. And my God will supply all your needs according to His glorious riches in Christ Jesus. (Phil. 4:17–18)

The gifts the Philippians gave to Paul are compared to offerings that were sacrificed by the temple priests and were pleasing to God—a concept used throughout the New Testament. Also, the Philippians' generosity would come back to them in the physical and spiritual blessings they would receive.

THE HOLY SPIRIT WILL COME TO US.

"But the helper, the Holy Spirit, whom the father will send in my name, he will teach you all things and bring to your remembrance all that I have said to you" (John 14:26).

We often use this passage to prove two things that are frequently taken out of context: 1) When Jesus left the earth, the Father sent the Holy Spirit to everyone. When we say "to everyone," we mean in the first century and now in our time. And 2) when the Holy Spirit comes, he will guide us in all things; or we will be led by the Spirit apart from the Spirit's own words. In other words, we will know what the Bible says in some manner other than by the sweat of our brow.

We may desire to make this passage say that the Spirit will guide us in some manner, but nowhere in the context of Jesus' speech does he mention you and me. From the context, we get that the intended audience of the speech were the twelve disciples. Let's broaden our scope and look at the surrounding verses that accompany this scripture.

One thing we want to remember in studying context is to first define the audience. To whom is the author speaking? If we go back to John 12:34, we get to a place where Jesus' speech was clearly for a different audience: "the crowd." Having established the prior audience in a different presentation, we can move forward to our intended target (John 13:1), the Father sending the Holy Spirit, and his intended purpose.

This is one place where the chapter break actually works in our favor. After Jesus' speech to the crowd, the subject changes from "the crowd" to the Passover supper. On a side note, the speech to the crowd came six days before the Last Supper (John 12:1). After that, John skips ahead to when Jesus rose from the supper to wash the attendees' feet. He first came to Simon Peter who gave Jesus a hard time about washing his feet (John 13:6). Then we read that Jesus washed the others' feet.

Seeing that he washed everyone's feet, we then know that the disciples were with Jesus at the Passover meal, but we must try not to assume that these were the disciples based on prior study. We must practice this exercise without assuming anything. It may not mean anything here in this passage, but I assure you that when we get to more difficult and complicated passages, we may go in the wrong direction. In verse 18, Jesus says, "I know whom I have chosen." *Now* we can refer back to previous scripture. We know Jesus has referred to his disciples as "those he chose." As we read through the passage, we come to another verse that leaves us with no doubt about his audience: "By this people will know that you are my disciples" (John 13:35).

So we have established the fact that Jesus is talking to his disciples. In the following verses, we now see both Thomas and Phillip asking Jesus questions. Then we move forward to the initial passage in question as we continue to read.

> These things I have spoken to you (*the disciples*) while I was still with you. But the helper, the Holy Spirit, whom the Father will send in my name, he will teach you all things and bring to your remembrance all that I have said to you. (John 14:25–26)

We may get the Holy Spirit. However, the only thing we can actually prove from these passages is that the disciples were the only ones promised the Holy Spirit at this time. Now does that mean I don't believe Christians receive the Holy Spirit? No, I'm only saying that in this context, Jesus isn't speaking to "the crowd" or us. We can only take what is taught to us in a collection of passages. Let other clear passages teach us what they may. Don't force Scripture out of its context.

SPEAKING IN TONGUES NOT GIBBERISH.

"And they (*the disciples*) were filled with the Holy Spirit and began to speak in other tongues" (Acts 2:4). This is the first passage in the Bible that mentions tongues.

The story begins with the coming of the day of Pentecost. The disciples were all together in one place. They had just finished selecting a disciple to replace Judas in Acts 1:21–26. Verse 21 tells us that these men were the ones who followed Jesus from his baptism by John the Baptist to when he was taken up (the ascension). They were witnesses of Jesus' resurrection. It was then that they began speaking in tongues.

There is no law that says we can't remember reading other scriptures or study and apply it to a previous passage to understand the study at hand. This is good exegesis. A good passage that illustrates this is 1 Corinthians 14:13: "Therefore, one who speaks in a tongue should pray that he can interpret." So we have just added interpretation to the mix, which would suggest that it could be possible for the speaker to interpret what was spoken in tongues to everyone.

Paul also mentions in the same context that there are many languages in the world and none without meaning. That helps us to understand that tongues must be interpreted, and they aren't meaningless languages.

If we go back to the book of Acts, we see the same concept:

> The multitude came together, and they were bewildered, because each one was hearing them speak in his own language. And they were amazed and astonished, saying . . . how is it we hear, each one in his own language? (Acts 2:6–8)

In conclusion, we can see how the Holy Spirit produced the ability for one to speak in a foreign language he didn't know so the foreign person who knew it could understand it.

We should be sure that we do not always use a microscope to examine the Scriptures. Most of the time, we use a wide-angle lens.

CHAPTER 4

THE RULE OF HISTORICAL INSIGHT

Don't separate interpretation from historical investigation.

The purpose of this rule is to serve as a constant reminder that the cultural milieu through the centuries is very complex. We cannot separate biblical truth from historical truth because they are intimately bound.

In interpreting, it is crucial to understand Hebrew, Egyptian, Persian, Babylonian, and Greek colloquial practices. Not to mention the people who lived in the Promised Land when the Israelites arrived to claim it. Also, the Canaanites of Joshua's time were the Philistines of Samson and David's time.

> WE CANNOT SEPARATE BIBLICAL TRUTH FROM HISTORICAL TRUTH.

The Bible makes a good start of this historical insight into the religious and cultural practices of these peoples. God wanted the Hebrew nation to be different. The reason God wanted the Israelites to keep themselves pure and only marry within their own race was so that God could fulfill his promise to Abraham: to bring the Messiah through his lineage.

> And if you are Christ's then you are Abraham's offspring, heirs according to promise. (Gal. 3:29)

The Messiah's work was to fix what man messed up. If we remember this truth, all of God's dealings in preserving his people will become clear. Jesus can't come through a broken seed line. So the historical context of Israel is bound to God's promise of salvation through Jesus. The point of God's promise to Abraham wasn't just a physical nation but a spiritual nation as well.

> And in your offspring shall all the nations of the earth be blessed, because you have obeyed my voice. (Gen. 22:18)

It is helpful to know the practices of these other cultures. The people Joshua was to drive out practiced idolatry. This practice would later cause Israel to fall away from the true God. These influences changed the Israelites' customs and behavior to the point that they quit serving God and worshiped the gods of those around them. This caused God to send Israel into exile in Babylon, where they were forced to reexamine their worldview.

We need to understand, as much as possible, the thoughts and belief systems of the people of a period and the events relevant to the overall scheme of redemption, presented through the whole Bible narrative. The Bible narrative has one goal: preserve the seed line from which the Messiah would be born, and

Chapter 4 · The Rule of Historical Insight

ultimately make a great spiritual nation of Christ followers. God dealt with Israel and the nations around them to do just that: preserve the seed line of Abraham. God would contain Israel one way or another to protect the seed of Abraham so the Messiah could come with atonement. This was why God instituted the law of Moses, to keep the people of Israel in check, for their own good and to preserve his plan of redemption.

Sometimes knowing a culture's food, whether eaten or forbidden, will give us insight into their religious practices. The Jews abstained from eating many animals because the old covenant forbids it. If we read the culinary laws in Leviticus with insight, we will see that God gave Israelites strict guidelines for what they ate or even touched.

When we take a close look at many of the prescribed practices, we see that God didn't strap the Jewish people with arbitrary, harsh rules. From Leviticus, we understand that God gave these rules to protect the Israelites from eating what they didn't know was bad for them. He was actually taking care of them. Ancient man wasn't ignorant by any means, but they lacked the scientific insight to have the medical knowledge we do today. Science and medicine were in their infancy during Biblical times. We understand that you don't eat diseased animals, touch dead things, or cut meat with a knife that you cut fish with a day ago. We wash it with soap and water. They could build a pyramid, but the Egyptians ate some pretty disgusting food.

When we read about Daniel and his friends telling their Babylonian handlers to let them eat vegetables and drink water instead of the king's dainties, we should, by deduction, realize that Babylonian food was not "what the doctor ordered" and violated the rules God gave Moses.

> But Daniel resolved that he would not defile himself with the king's food, or with the wine that he drank. (Dan. 1:8, ESV)

When we read of Peter telling God that he has never eaten the creepy crawlers in the bed sheet, we begin to understand that not only are the Levitical culinary laws passing away but, by metaphor, the Gentiles may receive the good news of salvation.

> [Peter] saw the heavens opened and something like a great sheet descending, being let down by its four corners upon the earth. In it were all kinds of animals and reptiles and birds of the air. And there came a voice to him: "Rise, Peter; kill and eat." But Peter said, "By no means, Lord; for I have never eaten anything that is common or unclean." (Acts 10:11–14, ESV)

The Gentiles were detestable to the Jews. As the Jews saw it, Gentiles were filthy beasts practicing detestable habits. However, God took an Old Testament culinary law and revealed to Peter that not only were the food laws going away but, as Jesus mentioned, so was the whole old covenant. The science wasn't going away. By the time Jesus announced his new covenant in the mid-first century, culinary knowledge had caught up. The Jews, by practice, had kept the law until it was common to do so. The Greek-Roman world, through insight, had finally learned what the Jews knew by their God-given laws. The life practices, habits, and knowledge the Canaanites possessed, so many years before Christ, were far inferior to the practices God revealed to the Israelites.

It might seem like a minute detail, but try to determine whether the cultural context of the passage at hand is basically

Jewish or Greco-Roman, or some combination of both. In some aspects, that minute detail may be quite large.

For the most part, the Gospels reflect Jewish backgrounds. For this reason, we can't overlook the fact that Jewish culture at that time cannot be removed from the cultural habits God instilled in them through the rules of the old Law.

However, all the Gospels have a Jewish/Gentile church or a Gentile mission as their ultimate audience. The Gospels should be looked at through the eyes of the Jew. Jesus made this clear when he stated, "I was sent only to the lost sheep of the house of Israel" (Matt. 15:21–28). It was later—after his ascension—that Jesus told Peter the Gentiles were invited into God's kingdom and sent Paul to the Greek world.

If we look back at the preceding paragraphs in Matthew, we see a Canaanite woman coming to Jesus and begging him to heal her daughter. Jesus' statement was a commitment to his mission.

> But she came and knelt before him, saying, "Lord, help me." And he answered, "It is not right to take the children's bread and throw it to the dogs." She said, "Yes, Lord, yet even the dogs eat the crumbs that fall from their masters' table." Then Jesus answered her, "O woman, great is your faith! Be it done for you as you desire." And her daughter was healed instantly. (Matt. 15:25–28)

The Gentiles' acceptance of a predominantly Jewish religion and worldview became their salvation.

We need to see the Gospels of Matthew, Mark, and John in the Old Testament. Also there is a need to place the Gospel of Luke within the Greek mindset of Theophilus (Luke's audience).

By understanding these two cultures, we can better understand how the Gospel traveled throughout the first-century world and the changes the Jew had to accept upon the arrival of the Gentile into the church.

We can see some cultural shifts at work in the Gospels themselves:

> And he called the people to him again and said to them, "Hear me, all of you, and understand: There is nothing outside a person that by going into him can defile him, but the things that come out of a person are what defile him." And when he had entered the house and left the people, his disciples asked him about the parable. And he said to them, "Then are you also without understanding? Do you not see that whatever goes into a person from outside cannot defile him, since it enters not his heart but his stomach, and is expelled?" (Thus he declared all foods clean.) And he said, "What comes out of a person is what defiles him. For from within, out of the heart of man, come evil thoughts, sexual immorality, theft, murder, adultery, coveting, wickedness, deceit, sensuality, envy, slander, pride, foolishness. All these evil things come from within, and they defile a person." (Mark 7:14–23)

The Jew was supposed to understand God's providence and care when, through Moses, God set up principles that would change his chosen people forever. They left Egypt as Egyptians in nature, but after forty years, they entered the Promised Land completely different people in practice and culture.

When Jesus speaks about almsgiving, divorce, oaths, etc., it is imperative to know Jewish culture on these points. But it would also be helpful to know the Greco-Roman views on such matters to understand the similarities or differences in these Gospels.

Likewise with Paul's epistles, it is especially important to have a feeling for Paul's own essential thoughts on the Jewish world. But because all of his letters were written to mostly Gentile churches situated in Greco-Roman culture, we must look for ways to understand that culture as well. The Jew and the Gentile came from completely different worlds as far as their experiences are concerned, so their metaphors, idioms, and other concepts of expression must be considered when examining any passage.

Our effort is to determine the meaning and significance of persons, places, events, institutions, concepts, or customs; a look into the culture of the peoples of the Bible. We need to know what they thought to understand how they reacted to the gospel.

A clear understanding of the Scriptures tells us that the books of Genesis through John were predominantly written to the Jews, and therefore yields a Jewish cultural experience. The books of Acts through Jude have a major Greco-Roman purpose. The exception is Revelation, which uses many Jewish idioms, metaphors, and figurative language—although Revelation was written for both Jew and Gentile Christians.

The purposes of a collection of texts may vary. Sometimes, as in the divorce passages, the purpose is to expose oneself to the various opinions, so as to see a clear picture. Such is the case with Jesus' answer to the Pharisees: "And Pharisees came up to him and tested him by asking, 'Is it lawful to divorce one's wife for any cause?'" (Matt. 19:3).

Jesus answered their tricky question with one of his own:

> "Have you not read that he who created them from the beginning made them male and female, and said,

> 'Therefore a man shall leave his father and his mother and hold fast to his wife, and the two shall become one flesh'? So they are no longer two but one flesh. What therefore God has joined together let not man separate." They said to him, "Why then did Moses command one to give a certificate of divorce and to send her away?" He said to them, "Because of your hardness of heart Moses allowed you to divorce your wives, but from the beginning it was not so. And I say to you: whoever divorces his wife, except for sexual immorality, and marries another, commits adultery." (Matt. 19:3–9)

The Pharisees came to Jesus with a question meant to trip him up. In the first century, there raged a debate among the Jews: could one divorce his wife for any reason or must you have the cause of unfaithfulness? The two schools of thought were two differing opinions of two different Jewish scholars and thus also their followers. Consequently, they wanted Jesus to take sides because they knew this would hamper his mission to one side or the other, causing division among the very people Jesus wanted to reach. Political thought may differ between then and today, but it still has the same effect: it divides.

Rather than getting tripped up, Jesus trips up the religious leaders by referring to God's natural order and why he created man to take a wife in the first place. Jesus taught a great truth about creation but avoided taking sides with the divisive leaders approaching him with ulterior motives. The Pharisees exploited the disagreement of thought that was a problem in the first century. Jesus went all the way back to the beginning and countered their argument.

Chapter 4 · The Rule of Historical Insight

The disciples misunderstood what was going on:

> The disciples said to him, "If such is the case of a man with his wife, it is better not to marry." But Jesus said to them, "Not everyone can receive this saying, but only those to whom it is given. For there are eunuchs who have been so from birth, and there are eunuchs who have been made eunuchs by men, and there are eunuchs who have made themselves eunuchs for the sake of the kingdom of heaven. Let the one who is able to receive this receive it." (Matt. 19:10–12)

The disciples got a good lesson in the difficulty of overcoming cultural pressures. Jesus' point here is that dedication to serving God as a single individual may be better than the perils of some getting married; for marriage isn't easy, and marriage isn't for everyone. In my years of providing marriage counseling I have come to realize that our own cultural pressure has convinced many to marry who shouldn't have done so.

The thing that drives culture is the complexity of thought. Common belief among both Jew and Gentile was their marriage bond. But their views on marriage and divorce varied greatly between the cultures. Jesus' point in giving them this advice was that his hearers would understand that dedication to God doesn't merely mean one should get married to serve God. By not marrying, one may serve him better.

Even Paul lets us know that he abstains from marriage for the gospel's sake: "Have we no right to eat and to drink? Have we no right to lead about a wife that is a believer, even as the rest of the apostles, and the brethren of the Lord, and Cephas?" (1 Cor. 9:4–5).

We need to understand the differences between the two audiences. Jesus was speaking to Jewish Pharisees who had lived under the Law's strict principles. Paul's letter was to the Gentile Corinthians, who lived in a city corrupt with pagan ideas and practices and were still held accountable for their actions. A sharp contrast in the question of accountability can be seen in Paul's letter to the Romans.

"For when the Gentiles, who do not have the law, by nature do what the law requires, they are a law unto themselves, even though they do not have the law" (Rom. 2:14).

Jesus' audience was all Jewish. This argument about marriage had been raging for centuries. Prior to the Mosaic Law, the Israelites spent four hundred years in Egypt. They had great cultural pressure to conform to ideas that were foreign to their ancestors. Before coming in contact with Egyptian culture and their polytheistic worldview, Joseph and his brothers and father were a nomadic people. From Abraham all the way to Joseph, God spoke directly to his people. Their nomadic lifestyle was simple with a simple relationship and dedication to God.

The major trouble Abraham experienced was: "Where is this heir that God promised?" It's clear that descendants (or the lack thereof) were the most important thing in his life. The marriage bond with Sarah and its purpose of procreation were his great concern. God promised Abraham children, and this promise included a host of generations from his seed.

Abraham also faced an opposing cultural problem in the cities of Sodom and Gomorrah where his nephew Lot lived. From firsthand experience, Abraham was aware that the cultural pressures from where masses gathered could form unhealthy choices. God was certainly aware of it and its tendency to pervert the natural order intended in marriage. Evil people corrupt good morals with their base desires and have an adverse effect on others. Even though Lot was a good man and hosted angels, he was willing to give up his daughters for an immoral purpose.

It is interesting to note that God set up this idea prior to Adam and Eve having children, which makes it all the more important. Adam and Eve had no parents to leave. But that didn't affect God's desire to establish the natural order of humanity.

By the time Paul wrote his letter to the Greek-speaking people of Corinth, huge differences had clashed between Greek and Hebrew culture and thought.

Around 332 BC, Alexander the Great had conquered the region of Judea. The Greeks brought a totally different view that contrasted with Jewish ideals—a Hellenistic view of the world that they considered superior to the Jewish way of life. The four hundred years of silence from God between the Old and New Testament brought with it a fight over the Jewish way of life in contrast with Greek culture. Alexander the Great and his desire to spread Hellenistic ideals caused not only great suffering to the Jews but also great difficulty for Paul. In his missionary journeys, Paul landed in the midst of the Greek worldview of the Corinthians. He spent most of his time explaining that God had a better way of life and salvation. And he met this culture head-on, which caused Paul great suffering, as well as all those who had turned to God.

In a world in turmoil Paul mentions how trusting the Lord and living differently secures your place in heaven. God wants us to lean on Jesus and be a light to this perverted world.

> Do all things without grumbling or disputing, that you may be blameless and innocent, children of God

without blemish in the midst of a crooked and twisted generation, among whom you shine as lights in the world. (Phil. 2:14–15)

Paul was always in danger but relied on the Lord to take care of him.

"Now I rejoice in my sufferings for your sake" (Col. 1:24) and "on frequent journeys, in . . . danger from robbers, danger from my own people, danger from Gentiles, danger in the city" (2 Cor. 11:26).

In between the Testaments—in four hundred years of God's silence—the Jews had been exposed to many nations' corrupt habits and wars. They only had their faith and Scriptures, not God's voice, to find comfort.

Both Jewish and Greek cultures had different worldviews—the gospel demanded that they change their mindset. Understanding these historical insights will help us understand the nuances of the differences and learn more perfectly the scriptures we study.

> UNDERSTANDING THESE HISTORICAL INSIGHTS WILL HELP US UNDERSTAND SCRIPTURE.

Another difference in cultural concept is the confusion over why (in our minds) Jesus was crucified on Friday afternoon and rose on Sunday morning; yet that doesn't add up to three days. In seeming contrast, in his own words Jesus claims something else: "Destroy this temple, and in three days I will raise it up" (John 2:19).

The Jews looked at a part of a day as constituting a full day—from 6 a.m. to 6 p.m. or dawn up to dusk was a whole day in any part. We look at a day as 12 a.m. to 12 a.m., so to rise on the third day would mean that Jesus would have to die at 12 a.m. on Friday and rise at 12 a.m. on Tuesday. The Jews didn't see it that way.

Hebrews would consider part of a day as the first day and part of Sunday as the third day. We should use caution to not put our modern-day spin on the three days and thus think the story is inaccurate. See how our cultural differences could confuse us?

For an overview of the political, religious, and intellectual ideals of first-century Judaism and Roman Hellenism, you may want to read one of the following: Eduard Lohse's *The New Testament Environment* or Everett Ferguson's *Backgrounds of Early Christianity*.

The complexity of the Greco-Roman side (Greece, Rome, and the provinces that were an amalgamation of all its customs) makes our study challenging but not impossible. With a little help from historical insight, we can understand the cultural norms of the people of the old covenant and the first-century new covenant.

CHAPTER 5

THE RULE OF RELEVANCE

Having a bearing on or connection with the matter at hand. Meaningful or purposeful in current society or culture.

If we are to understand relevance as part of how we study and apply Scripture, we must first understand three facts:

- First, Jesus was the last purveyor of Old Testament fulfillment, purpose, and relevance.
- Second, New Testament revelation, purpose, and fulfillment were confined to the first century.
- Third, after the first century concludes, the entirety of Scripture, both in meaning and practice for us, has its basis in history and history alone.

If the matter at hand isn't relevant to the person hearing what is being spoken, then our understanding of the matter is wrong. It is entirely illogical to assume that any matter being presented has an ounce of relevance if it is meaningless, in a practical application, to the person the matter is addressing. That is to say, something said to me with no bearing on my life is irrelevant. If you told me that the weather in Spain was balmy and wet, that would have no relevance to me if I lived in West Texas where it is dry and over a hundred degrees.

Let's look at a specific passage:

"Take care not to go up into the mountain or touch the edge of it. Whoever touches the mountain shall be put to death" (Exod. 19:12).

If I read this scripture, would I assume that I shouldn't go hiking in the mountains? Or better yet, that I shouldn't go to Sinai and hike on that mountain? No, the story of Israel at Mount Sinai is just a story to me at first reading. It is not relevant to me. But when I read Hebrews, I might see that this verse has more personal relevance:

> For you have not come to what may be touched, a blazing fire and darkness and gloom and a tempest and the sound of a trumpet and a voice whose words made the hearers beg that no further messages be spoken to them. For they could not endure the order that was given, "If even a beast touches the mountain, it shall be stoned." Indeed, so terrifying was the sight that Moses said, "I tremble with fear." But you have come to Mount Zion and to the city of the living God, the heavenly Jerusalem, and to innumerable angels in festal gathering, and to the assembly of the firstborn who are enrolled in heaven, and to God, the judge of all, and to the spirits of the righteous made perfect, and to Jesus, the mediator of a new covenant, and

to the sprinkled blood that speaks a better word than the blood of Abel. (Heb. 12:18–24)

We can understand that the sight the Israelites came to was much different than what the book of Hebrews tells its readers about the mountain they came to. One mountain was ominous and forbidden to approach; the other was inviting and approachable. In this explanation, we can see that Hebrews applies to us so much more than the Exodus account of Sinai applies.

Let's jump ahead for clarity's sake so that we can see the relevance of the differences between the salvation offered to the Israelites' old covenant relationship at Mount Sinai and the new covenant offered to us at Mount Zion. Hebrews states that we have come to Mount Zion, which is equated to coming to the new covenant relationship with God:

"Jesus *is* the mediator of a new covenant, and to the sprinkled blood that speaks a better word than the blood of Abel" (Heb. 12:24).

We also can reach back to Jesus' statement in Matthew: "For this is my blood of the covenant, which is poured out for many for the forgiveness of sins" (Matt. 26:28).

So now we have a mountain the Israelites couldn't approach or they would die compared to a mountain we can approach where there is life. The covenant, which was made to the Israelites, had the sacrifice of animals. "For it is impossible for blood of bulls and goats to take away sins" (Heb. 10:4).

We should understand that the relationship the Israelites had with God is not relevant to us; it is historical now. We may *learn* something from history, but we can never *live* it. The new covenant is an everlasting covenant, which is completely relevant to us and how we are to live. Likewise, to the Greek Christians in the first century, Sinai would not be relevant to them, but the good news of the gospel would. Especially to the Gentiles who were never under the Jewish law. For this reason, Paul would condemn Jews coming to Galatia and telling the Gentile Christians there that they must be circumcised.

> For even those who are circumcised do not themselves keep the law, but they desire to have you circumcised that they may boast in your flesh. . . . For neither circumcision counts for anything, nor uncircumcision, but a new creation. (Gal. 6:13–15)

We have a covenant with God through Christ, which removes sin and gives life to those who come near.

> For since the law was but a shadow of the good things to come instead of the true form of these realities, it can never, by the same sacrifices that are continually offered every year, make perfect those who draw near. Otherwise, would they not have ceased to be offered, since the worshipers, having once been cleansed, would no longer have any consciousness of sins? But in these sacrifices there is a reminder of sins every year. For it is impossible for the blood of bulls and goats to take away sins. . . . He does away with the first in order to establish the second. And by that will we have been sanctified through the offering of the body of Jesus Christ once for all. (Heb. 10:1–10)

So we see that the mountain at Sinai was unapproachable before Jesus, and that the mountain of Zion is now approachable through the blood of Jesus' sacrifice. That approachability is relevant to us in contrast to Sinai. The old Law was relevant

Chapter 5 · The Rule of Relevance

to pre-Christ followers of God versus post-Christ followers of God. It's a matter of historical relevance; pre-Christ is relevant to the Jew only, and post-Christ has historical relevance to us as followers of Jesus.

Old Testament sacrifice was relevant as a way to postpone the judgment of the sins of Israel, which pushes sin into the future. But the relevance now is that Jesus, the mediator of a new covenant, can forgive sin now.

Error and truth are found in a simple concept. If I were walking down the street one day and picked up a letter addressed to Elmo Gunther on the sidewalk, I should conclude that it was not written to me. However, I open the letter and read it. Aunt Betty says she's coming to see Elmo in one month. I immediately prepare for Aunt Betty's arrival. While I prepare for her arrival, certain things nag at me and my reasoning, which somehow gets suppressed. I know for certain that my family has never mentioned an Aunt Betty. And I don't really have an Aunt Betty. The letter's postmark indicates that it was sent three weeks and four days ago. So I need to hurry to the grocery store to find something to prepare. Aunt Betty will probably be hungry when she gets here. Then I realize, will it be a long trip? Wanting and desiring to be a good nephew, I go back and search for the answer. I live in LA, and my newfound aunt lives in Dallas.

Oh my, it will be a long trip. And if that is not enough, I don't know if I am supposed to pick up Aunt Betty at the airport or the train station. Now I'm in a panic. I don't know what is required of me. So I suffer the consequences of my newfound belief. But in the back of my mind, I have this nagging feeling that I can never reconcile this kind of thinking with real relevance. If it doesn't have relevance, don't be afraid to look elsewhere. It's better to start over than to keep piling more Scripture on to rationalize irrelevance.

We all have been there as new converts. The Bible tells us to do something, and we try and try to live out its importance in our lives. Because we know it's necessary. We have a desire to understand God and put what we learn into practice. If we don't have rules to guide us, then we can easily be duped into error because we can't recognize the truth. Truth is always relevant to the hearer. If it is not, then it is a lie.

> TRUTH IS ALWAYS RELEVANT TO THE HEARER.

Let's consider more differences between the Law God gave to the Israelites at Mount Sinai under Moses and the Law Jesus declared he would establish at his death through his blood. Which is relevant to us? If we say we should practice the Sabbath rest prescribed in Old Testament Law but are not sacrificing animals required by that Law, are we not breaking the Law?

"So if you are offering your gift at the altar and there remember that your brother has something against you, leave your gift there before the altar and go. First be reconciled to your brother, and then come and offer your gift" (Matt. 5:23–24).

"This is the law for her who bears a child, either male or female. And if she cannot afford a lamb, then she shall take two turtledoves or two pigeons, one for a burnt offering and the other for a sin offering. And the priest shall make atonement for her, and she shall be clean" (Lev. 12:7–8).

These sacrifices were required by the Old Testament. So why, if we want to be good Christians, aren't we killing and burning pigeons? Why don't women who are giving birth offer doves by bringing them to the priest? Why don't we have priests? Where is the temple?

The simple answer is: Jesus told Jews of his day to sacrifice. Jesus lived and died under the Old Testament. He shed his blood to make a new covenant. The old covenant is relevant to those who lived under it. The new covenant is relevant to those who live under it. The rules of one do not cross over to the other.

There is a major shift in relevance. Under the old Law, the Jew wasn't sanctified until the future. The Day of Atonement was always putting off sins to the future for those who lived under the old covenant. It was a cleansing of the flesh. Under Christ, we are purified from the inside out. There is Christ's blood that atones forever and not the blood of animals, which only postponed sin for another year. In explaining his work, Jesus looks forward to his death, the single most important event in history.

"Not that the testimony that I receive is from man, but I say these things so that you may be saved. . . . You search the Scriptures because you think that in them you have eternal life; and it is they that bear witness about me" (John 5:34, 39).

Salvation in the Old Testament always included a forward look. The author of Hebrews explains it this way from an Old Testament perspective. He explains the "look forward" to Jesus in the Old Testament, contrasting the "look back" at Jesus' work in the New.

> For if the blood of goats and bulls, and the sprinkling of defiled persons with the ashes of a heifer, sanctify for the purification of the flesh, how much more will the blood of Christ, who through the eternal Spirit offered himself without blemish to God, purify our conscience from dead

> works to serve the living God. Therefore he is the mediator of a new covenant, so that those who are called may receive the promised eternal inheritance. (Heb 9:13–15)

We must always remember that there was an Old Testament Jesus who was relevant to the Old Testament Jew. Those are prophesies of the coming Messiah, his life. But then there is the New Testament Jesus who was raised from the grave and atones for all now.

The Scripture must always be relevant to the persons spoken to, or our interpretation is wrong.

CHAPTER 6

THE RULE OF PRECEDENTS

We must not create new usage for a word or concept which has been previously established.

Just as a judge's chief occupation is the study of previous cases, so must the interpreter use precedents to determine whether they really support an alleged doctrine. Consider the Bereans who were called "noble" because they searched the Scriptures to determine if what Paul taught them was true. The Bereans looked for precedents in determining truth in the things Paul was speaking. They looked over what had been previously written to analyze Paul's teaching as genuine.

> THE INTERPRETER USES PRECEDENTS.

> The brothers immediately sent Paul and Silas away by night to Berea, and when they arrived they went into the Jewish synagogue. Now these Jews were more noble than those

in Thessalonica; they received the word with all eagerness, examining the Scriptures daily to see if these things were so. (Acts 17:10–11)

In a simple exercise, we could concentrate on verses that say, "For this reason" or "Have you not read?" Jesus often used precedents. He used precedents to answer a question the Pharisees asked about divorce:

And Pharisees came up to him and tested him by asking, "Is it lawful to divorce one's wife for any cause?" He answered, "Have you not read that he who created them from the beginning made them male and female, and said, 'Therefore a man shall leave his father and his mother and hold fast to his wife, and the two shall become one flesh'? So they are no longer two but one flesh. What therefore God has joined together let not man separate." (Matt. 19:3–6)

In saying, "Have you not read," he was appealing to a precedent set by God's natural order of creation: "Therefore a man shall leave his father and his mother and hold fast to his wife, and they shall become one flesh" (Gen. 2:24).

Jesus often appealed to past statements to give validity to his teachings.

On a Sabbath, while he was going through the grain fields, his disciples plucked and ate some heads of grain, rubbing them in their hands. But some of the Pharisees said, "Why are you doing what is not lawful to do on the Sabbath?" And Jesus answered them, "Have you not read what David did when he was hungry, he and those who were with him: how he entered the house of God and took and ate the bread of the Presence, which is not lawful for any but the priests to eat, and also gave it to those with him?" And he said to them, "The Son of Man is lord of the Sabbath." (Luke 6:1–5)

The Pharisees were quite legalistic and saw the Law as restrictive. But Jesus saw the spirit of the Law as a parent being protective. Jesus saw that the primary reason for God's creation of the Sabbath was to help the Israelites understand that they needed to rest from their labor. The precedent of God resting after six days of work was the basis of Jesus' teaching. God rested on Saturday; now you rest on Saturday. The Sabbath was meant to be a gift, not a burden as the Pharisees taught. So when Jesus' followers were hungry and ate, just as David did, Jesus had no problem with them eating on the Sabbath.

He had to teach this way often because the Pharisees (legalistic religious leaders) were teaching error. This is why Jesus answered them, appealing to what they had gotten wrong because they didn't or wouldn't apply precedent correctly.

In teaching the truth about the Sabbath, Jesus, speaking of David, appealed to sensible thinking, which the Pharisees were certainly not practicing. In the precedent, God didn't have a problem with David. Why should they have a problem with Jesus' disciples?

Jesus often used precedents to argue the truth. Consider his comments:

> But when the chief priests and the scribes saw the wonderful things that he did, and the children (were) crying out in the temple, "Hosanna to the Son of David!"

> they were indignant, and they said to him, "Do you hear what these (*children*) are saying?" And Jesus said to them, "Yes; have you never read, 'Out of the mouths of infants and nursing babies you have prepared praise'?" (Matt. 21:15–16)

After telling the story of the parable of the tenants, Jesus mentioned how the religious leaders would reject the Messiah. He stated: "Did you never read in the Scriptures: 'The stone that the builders rejected has become the cornerstone; this was the Lord's doing, and it is marvelous in our eyes'?" (Matt. 21:42).

Sometimes precedent is proven by a broader view of the Scriptures, as is prominent in Jesus' statement:

> You search the Scriptures because you think that in them you have eternal life; and it is they that bear witness about me, yet you refuse to come to me that you may have life. I do not receive glory from people. But I know that you do not have the love of God within you. I have come in my Father's name, and you do not receive me. If another comes in his own name, you will receive him. How can you believe, when you receive glory from one another and do not seek the glory that comes from the only God? Do not think that I will accuse you to the Father. There is one who accuses you: Moses, on whom you have set your hope. For if you believed Moses, you would believe me; for he wrote of me. But if you do not believe his writings, how will you believe my words? (John 5:39–47)

Here we get a clue about precedents; Moses prophesied about Jesus fourteen hundred years before he came. So the pattern of Christ's authority was set by these prophesies in that the

Old Testament spoke often of one coming who would be like their leader, Moses. The Messiah would be this person of whom Moses prophesied. God spoke to Moses and said:

> I will raise up for them a prophet like you from among their brothers. And I will put my words in his mouth, and he shall speak to them all that I command . . . And whoever will not listen to my words that he shall speak in my name, I myself will require it of him. (Deut. 18:18–19)

So in the Old Testament prophesies, by precedents, we can also conclude that Moses and Elijah are the same person: Jesus.

> Remember the law of my servant Moses, the statutes and rules that I commanded him at Horeb for all Israel. Behold, I will send you Elijah the prophet before the great and awesome day of the LORD comes. And he will turn the hearts of fathers to their children and the hearts of children to their fathers, lest I come and strike the land with a decree of utter destruction. (Mal. 4:5–6)

Precedent should always be considered while trying to draw out the meaning of any passage or concept presented by the Scriptures.

CHAPTER 7

THE RULE OF UNITY

The part of Scripture being interpreted must be construed with reference to the significance of the whole. An interpretation must be consistent with the rest of Scripture.

When we study the words, phrases, or concepts in the Bible, we need to make sure that what we determine is true in one area will not contradict what we read in some other part of Scripture.

As students of the Bible, we must understand that its author, the Holy Spirit, expects us to remember what went before as we progress through the whole Bible. There is not enough space in the world for the Spirit to explain things to us over and over again. The Scripture that is coming ahead builds on the Scripture that went before.

For example, we can't have sin be sin in the Garden of Eden, and sin be something altogether different later in Scripture. Destroy the definition of sin and you lose the whole narrative of the Bible. If sin in the Garden isn't sin in our lives, then we can excuse our behavior as relative to a fiat standard created in a delusional idealism. Even our very thoughts become benign. That is to say: we become deluded and somewhat mentally ill if we think we can improve our lives with anything short of God's redemption. If sin is to be relevant at all, then it must be relevant to us in the same way it was relevant to Adam and Eve. The definition of sin can't change from the Garden to us, or the unity of the Scripture is broken.

If we question the unity of the Scriptures, we question the legitimacy of Jesus and his apostles to really wield authority. If sin is not a unified concept in the whole of Scripture, it is not dangerous at all, and Jesus and the apostles become liars. If we don't see it that way, it's because of our lack of understanding of the unity in the Bible narrative.

Rebellion (*sin*) against God set in motion the need for a savior, which logically produced the narrative of the whole Bible. By understanding unity, we can understand the definition of sin being the same in the Garden of Eden and when Jesus and the apostles walked the earth. Indeed, if the definition of sin was the same for four thousand years, it is therefore, by precedent and the lack of new revelation, the same today, no matter what we rationalize to be sin. We can understand sin being sin because Moses and the apostles Matthew and John corroborate this fact. Here is how we understand that this is true through the rule of unity.

The unity between several passages on a subject can give us a clearer view of what the Holy Spirit intended.

In 1 John 2:16 we read, "For all that is in the world—the desires of the flesh and the desires of the eyes and pride of life—is not from the Father but is from the world."

John declares that there are three areas by which we can fall into sin (*failure to reproduce God's holiness in our lives*). These areas include 1) our failure to avoid and resist temptation; 2) our failure to master the desires of our flesh (*greed, consummation, lasciviousness, etc.*) or the desires or our eyes (*covetousness*); and 3) the pride of life (*assuming we are the god of our own destiny*).

> THE UNITY BETWEEN PASSAGES CAN GIVE US A CLEARER VIEW.

Let's look at two examples of temptation in these three areas of sin.

First, the temptation of Jesus: "Then Jesus was led up by the Spirit into the wilderness to be tempted by the devil. And after fasting forty days and forty nights, he was hungry. And the tempter came and said to him, 'If you are the Son of God, command these stones to become loaves of bread.' But he answered, 'It is written, "Man shall not live by bread alone, but by every word that comes from the mouth of God."' Then the devil took him to the holy city and set him on the pinnacle of the temple and said to him, "If you are the Son of God, throw yourself down, for it is written, "'He will command his angels concerning you,' and "'On their hands they will bear you up, lest you strike your foot against a stone.'"

Jesus said to him, "Again it is written, 'You shall not put the Lord your God to the test.'" Again, the devil took him to a very high mountain and showed him all the kingdoms of the world and their glory. And he said to him, "All these I will give you, if you will fall down and worship me." Then Jesus said to him, "Be gone, Satan! For it is written, "'You shall worship the Lord your God and him only shall you serve.'" Then the devil left him, and behold, angels came and were ministering to him" (Matthew 4:1–11).

Notice the three areas in which Jesus was tempted.

First, the tempter appealed to Christ's hunger:

"The tempter came and said to him, 'If you are the Son of God, command these stones to become loaves of bread.'"

The tempter tempted Jesus with the "lust of the flesh" (I deserve whatever I crave).

"Then the devil took him to the holy city and set him on the pinnacle of the temple and said to him, 'If you are the Son of God, throw yourself down, for it is written, 'He will command his angels concerning you'" (Matt. 4:5–6).

The devil tried to get Jesus to fail God by tempting him with "the pride of life" (I deserve to be better than any other).

In the last attempt to get Jesus to sin: "Again, the devil took him to a very high mountain and showed him all the kingdoms of the world and their glory. And he said to him, 'All these I will give you, if you will fall down and worship me'" (Matt. 4:8–9).

The "lust of the eye" (I deserve to own all that I see).

We should note here that people don't come to hate God because of what "he is," but what they desire that he doesn't give them. Even the ungodly feel that God should serve them.

Second, John's explanation of sin goes all the way back to the Garden and the tempting of Eve by the snake:

> Now the serpent was more crafty than any other beast of the field that the Lord God had made. He said to the woman: "Did God actually say, 'You shall not eat of any tree in the garden'?" And the woman said to the serpent, "We may eat of the fruit of the trees in the garden, but God said, 'You shall not eat of the fruit of the tree that is

in the midst of the garden, neither shall you touch it, lest you die.'" But the serpent said to the woman, "You will not surely die. For God knows that when you eat of it your eyes will be opened, and you will be like God, knowing good and evil." So when the woman saw that the tree was good for food, and that it was a delight to the eyes, and that the tree was to be desired to make one wise, she took of its fruit and ate, and she also gave some to her husband who was with her, and he ate. (Gen. 3:1–6, ESV)

Eve was tempted in the same three areas that Jesus was:

So when Eve saw that the tree was "good for food," she was tempted with the lust of the flesh.

Also, she looked at the fruit and noticed in her heart that it was a delight to the eyes. She was tempted by the lust of the eye (*covetousness*).

Next, she fell to the pride of life. She traded her humility, when in her heart she saw that the tree was to be desired to make one wise. She desired to be like God in a way he never intended.

The unity of the Scriptures gives us a universal understanding of sin. The definition of sin has never changed throughout the Bible narrative and will never change—ever. It's set in stone.

The narrative of the Scriptures begins with sin, and the need for a savior finds its pivotal point in the death and resurrection of Jesus. Then the narrative goes through the New Testament, providing salvation for sin by the spreading of the good news and the righteousness of Jesus—transferred to us through his new covenant, in his blood (see Matthew 26:28).

If sin shifts its meaning throughout the Bible, then Paul wouldn't have been able to say with any certainty: "For our sake he made him (Jesus) to be sin who knew no sin, so that in him we might become the righteousness of God" (2 Cor. 5:21).

There is no sin that falls outside of these three areas, as John declared, "All that is in the world—the desires of the flesh and the desires of the eyes and pride of life—is not from the father but is from the world" (1 John 2:16). When we look at sin, there is usually one area of sin we fail in more than another. Is it the lust of the flesh, the lust of the eye, or the pride of life?

How can we overcome these three areas of sin and be more righteous? Matthew 5:20 is Jesus' preface to the Sermon on the Mount, and the sermon shows how to exceed the righteousness of the scribes and Pharisees. It's kind of a different version than we are used to. We would understand it better if he had said, "Let me tell you how you can be more righteous than your religious leaders."

"For I tell you, unless your righteousness exceeds that of the scribes and Pharisees, you will never enter the kingdom of heaven" (Matt. 5:20).

Jesus' sermon gives us hope of being able to keep the areas of sin at bay in our lives. He teaches us how to pray and how important it is to stay in communion with God, how we honor him as God, never contradicting the unity of his purpose.

The unity of the Bible is the amazing accomplishment of the Holy Spirit's work. Though Jesus' sermon had a specific audience under the Jewish national covenant, it proves true in its unity and practical application two thousand years after Scripture fell silent.

Paul wrote to Timothy, specifically saying, "All Scripture is breathed out by God and profitable for teaching, for reproof, for correction, and for training in righteousness, that the man of God may be complete, equipped for every good work" (2 Tim. 3:16–17).

Timothy had heard these Scriptures all his life. The Scriptures that Paul was referring to were the books of Genesis through Malachi. The New Testament was only being written. The letters Timothy received were only two of the letters that would ultimately become the New Testament. Paul was confident that what Timothy had studied all his life was unified in such a way that he would understand perfectly what Paul was saying.

Apologist Tim Chaffey writes: "The Bible is unlike any other religious book. Despite forty authors writing from three continents over nearly two thousand years, it maintains a perfect consistency of message. Its words point unerringly to Christ, whose work on the cross was ordained by God—the true author of the Bible—before the world began."[1]

Apologist Patrick Zukeran reminds us: "The Bible was written over 1,500 years, by forty different authors, at different places, under various circumstances, and addressing a multitude of issues—it is amazing that with such diversity, there is such unity in the Bible. That unity is organized around one theme: God's redemption of man and all of creation. Hundreds of controversial subjects are addressed, and yet the writers do not contradict each other. The Bible is an incredible document."[2]

We have in the Bible a book that can test anyone or any doctrine. If it doesn't fall in line with the Bible's unity, it fails the test of sound doctrine.

---

1. Tim Chaffey, "Unity of the Bible," *Answers Magazine*, April 1, 2011.
2. Patrick Zukeran, "The Authority of the Bible," Probe Ministries, August 30, 2014, probe.org/authority-of-the-bible-a-strong-argument-for-christianity.

CHAPTER 8

THE RULE OF INFERENCE

An inference is a fact reasonably deduced from another fact.

There is no place in the New Testament writings that actually say the two men who were crucified on either side of Jesus died. We assume they did, but that fact is never stated. Thus, we might refer to this belief as a "logical inference," and few would argue with us. However, it would be an assumption to use guesswork to interpret Scripture.

Let's examine this story to see what we can learn.

> Two others, who were criminals, were also led away to be executed with Jesus. . . . One of the criminals who hung there heaped abuse on Him. "Are you not the Christ?" he said. "Save yourself and us!" But the other one rebuked him, saying, "Do you not even fear God, since you are under the same judgment? We are punished justly, for we are receiving what our actions deserve. But this man has

done nothing wrong." Then he said, "Jesus, remember me when you come into your kingdom!" And Jesus said to him, "Truly I tell you, today you will be with me in Paradise." (Luke 23:32, 39–42)

The fact that two men hung on crosses is stated. The idea that they died is an assumption.

In interpreting the Scriptures, we must not make assumptions. Assumptions can be true in the way a broken clock is right twice a day. Assuming that something is true does not make it true.

> IN INTERPRETING THE SCRIPTURES, WE MUST NOT MAKE ASSUMPTIONS.

Assumptions are always filled with bias and previously conceived information. Assumptions lead to dogma and practices not proven in Scripture. It should be our intention, in studying these rules, to get as far away from assumptions as possible.

Keep in mind that facts are seldom facts, but what people think are facts, heavily tinged with assumptions.

Our challenge is to shed our preconceived opinions, biases, and assumptions to honestly learn the truth. If we don't continuously reexamine what we think to be true, we may not find what the truth is. The one thing to remember in approaching the Scriptures is: "You don't know what you don't know."

To understand Scripture is to examine all available facts and draw a logical conclusion. As far as inference is concerned, we can't infer something in the absence of all the facts we can muster. The fact that most that were hung on a cross died does

CHAPTER 8 · THE RULE OF INFERENCE

not prove that the two men beside Jesus died. We need more factual evidence.

It is a fact that Jesus told one of the men that he would be with him that day in a place he called Paradise. We can't infer what Paradise is because, in this passage, there is no more evidence or explanation of Paradise to come to any kind of conclusion. To infer something takes more than one piece of stated evidence. We would have to look elsewhere for corroborating evidence about Paradise.

We can know the fate of at least one of these men by what is inferred.

Simply put, we know Jesus died. In a later part of the story of the crucifixion we read: "Then Jesus called out in a loud voice, 'Father, into your hands I commit My Spirit.' And when He had said this, He breathed His last" (Luke 23:46).

We know Jesus died because we know that if you cease to breathe, you die. Having established that Jesus died, we can move on to our next fact: Jesus said, "Truly I tell you, today you will be with me in Paradise."

So we know that Jesus died, and we know that he told the one thief that he would go with him to Paradise. With those two facts we can infer that for the thief to go with Jesus, he would have to die. To us, the fact that Jesus died can lead to a solid conclusion that the thief Jesus spoke to also died.

How do we know that the other thief died?

If we examine verse 32, we see the thieves' sentence mentioned: "Two others, who were criminals, were also led away to be executed with Jesus" (Luke 23:32).

We have proven the fate of one of the thieves. We can assume that because the Roman soldiers were very efficient in carrying out crucifixion orders, the other thief died too. However, we are still left with an assumption, albeit a very good one. Based on history, we can conclude with a fair amount of certainty that the other thief died.

An interesting point here is to realize that if we had no "historical insight" into the abilities of the Roman soldiers to execute prisoners (from extra-biblical documents), we wouldn't be able to make this reasonable assumption. This would put us in what is called "negative inference."

Negative inference happens when an interpreter takes a statement of fact and then assumes that the negative premise is equally true. Negative inference usually shows up when we take one fact and erroneously conclude that the assumption is indeed a fact: the one thief died—therefore both died.

In this case, what we would be left with is a wild and unsubstantiated guess. We should understand that negative inference or guesswork is never the truth.

To treat your facts with imagination is one thing; to imagine your facts is another thing.

The Rule of Inference is a powerful tool if we wield it correctly.

CHAPTER 9

THE RULE OF LOGIC

A probable set of conclusions based on facts

In the search for understanding the Scriptures, we need to always remember that "we don't know what we don't know." So the challenge is to reexamine everything we think we know against the possibility that we may be wrong before we're right.

The only way we can achieve a more exact, more complete mastery of the Bible is to test everything we feel is true against what we can prove with logical progression. Sometimes we only see what we want, not what we need. The process of logical conclusions based on evidence tells us what we need to see.

Logic is a deep and confusing subject to most. I don't intend nor purport to teach you logic here. However, you don't have to know formal studies in logic to understand Scripture. Scripture is very logical. Paul's progression of logical thought presented in the book of Romans would, I believe, fascinate Aristotle himself. Understanding how to follow Scripture logically will help you separate truth from fabrication. The more you absorb, the more you will be able to recognize false teaching. Paul said that with the unity of the faith and of the knowledge of the son of God, we won't be: "tossed to and fro and carried around by every wind of teaching and cunning, in the craftiness of men with a view to the scheming of deceit" (Eph. 4:14). We shouldn't be fooled. If it happened then, it happens now. Human nature hasn't changed.

Jesus said, "The truth will set you free," but the truth can only set us free when we know it to be true—not what we *feel* is true.

The Hebrew writer said, "Faith is the things hoped for the evidence of things not seen" (Heb. 11:1).

The key word here is "evidence." We need to trust what we can prove, not what we desire or assume to be true. For what we desire, what our emotions control, is deceiving, but what we can prove is solid. If we trust our feelings before logic, we have no basis on which to know the unseen. We rely on logic to prove what we must feel. God created man's ability to think, so we should.

> WE NEED TO TRUST WHAT WE CAN PROVE, NOT WHAT WE DESIRE OR ASSUME TO BE TRUE.

The radio show host and writer Dennis Prager says: "The only thing that people share is reason and evidence. If the laws of reason, logic, and evidence are suspended, then dialogue is absolutely 100 percent useless."

In interpreting the Scriptures, we must see before we believe—not believe before we see. Miracles are one of the things Christians struggle with the most. We don't look at miracles logically and bring their reason and purpose to their logical conclusion. We stop at the vague notion that somehow it is wise to say, "If you had faith, you would believe in miracles."

God didn't run around throwing a miracle out here and there just for fun. Nothing God does is without reason and purpose.

Logic is linear. We follow a set of facts that brings us to a conclusion. Illogic is circular—we follow a set of suppositions to come to a predisposed idea: wishful thinking. If I take the presupposition that "the universe is so expansive we can't be alone," then it wouldn't be so far off to think that "UFOs are alien spacecraft." "Because we are not alone" gives rise to circular thinking. We are not alone, therefore aliens are visiting us; ergo, aliens are visiting us because the universe is vast. The problem is not that there's intelligent life visiting us from the vastness of space. Rather, the question is, "Can life visit us from the vastness of space?"

For argument's sake, let's say that one could travel at the speed of light. I'll give you that. NASA has stated that the nearest planet that could possibly sustain life is fourteen light-years away. Physically, then, it would take one alien fourteen years, traveling at the speed of light, to reach earth. After they reached earth, they would fly around and mess with us in the backwoods and fly back home. Now this is pedantic, but the example of circular thinking stands. What's the reason? What's the purpose?

The problem is reason and purpose. Nothing is done without reason and purpose.

In life, we realize that a child is born. We know that for a fact. We see it happen. What we don't know is by what mysterious reason an embryo starts from a few cells and develops into a child. Now with science, we can watch an embryo grow. That doesn't tell us any more than we knew before about how it happens. It's just an observation. What we can know is that the purpose of an embryo is to get one thing to its finished product.

So though we can't understand how it happens, we understand from observation that it does happen. In the end, we know that a baby is the reason for and the end result of the embryo. We know for a fact that a child is born from an embryo and that not knowing how it happens isn't the point. Rather, knowing the "reason" is the point.

Miracles are a little like an embryo. The reason we haven't yet become comfortable with miracles and the resurrection isn't because we don't believe, but because we don't understand their purpose. The end result of an embryo is a child. But what is the end result of a miracle?

We get caught up in the actual miracle itself instead of the logical reason for a miracle. Once proven, a reason doesn't have to prove itself over and over. We may be afraid to give up miracles not because we don't believe but because we aren't sure. Once sure of the reason and the purpose, we can let the miraculous find its place in history. The unseen world still exists; it just doesn't have to prove itself to every generation continually.

Once a hypothesis is proven, it needs no other verification. Once miracles serve their purpose, there is no need for them to continue.

We discussed the definition of a biblical miracle in Chapter 1, the "Rule of Definition." In the rest of this chapter, we will logically deduce the purpose of a miracle.

In review, we learned that a miracle must contain three elements. These three elements come primarily from the book of Acts.

First, there must be a sign outside the realm of the physical universe, such as healing a man's severed ear like Jesus did on the night of his betrayal. Second, everyone present is witness to the man's ear being healed. And third, those presently standing there couldn't deny that it happened.

Let's analyze this through a couple of passages. An incident took place between Peter and the priests who wanted Peter to stop talking about Jesus (Acts 4:13–18). The key to this passage is verse 16 where unbelieving Jews make a pronouncement about what a biblical miracle really was: "'What shall we do with these men?' they asked. 'For that a notable sign has been performed through them is evident to all the inhabitants of Jerusalem, and we cannot deny it'" (Acts 4:16).

These are our three qualifications for biblical miracles:

- It is clear to everyone standing there (everyone witnesses the sign)
- A notable or remarkable sign has occurred (a man is healed in an unnatural way)
- We cannot deny it

The Sanhedrin court had a problem. The man who was healed was in their presence, and they couldn't very well deny that. He made a great witness!

"But seeing the man who was healed standing beside them, they had nothing to say in opposition" (Acts 4:14).

Now we have seen that through three facts we have a probable conclusion. That's how logic works. Though we can't see how a miracle works, we can see what it produces. Just like we don't know how an embryo works, but we know what it produces: a child. So we took a set of facts and deduced a conclusion. And that conclusion is that miracles did exist.

Now let's look at why miracles were necessary. In Acts 2:22, we see the same pattern: "Men of Israel, hear these words: Jesus of Nazareth, a man attested to you by God with mighty works and wonders and signs that God did through him in your midst, as you yourselves know" (Acts 2:22).

However, we have a different element in this verse than the others. It is this: "Jesus . . . a man *attested* to you by God . . . did through *him*." God showed his approval through miracles that Jesus was the Messiah—his son.

When we see that God produces miracles through Jesus as a way of showing his approval or attestation, we can logically conclude that a miracle is a way for God to let people know the performer was approved—from him.

The NIV translates it this way: "was a man accredited by God to you by miracles, wonders and signs." The Berean Study Bible translates the passage: "was a man certified by God to you by miracles, wonders, and signs, which God did among you through Him."

Whether translated "attested," "certified," or "approved," the result is the same. No matter which Bible translation you prefer, the reason for miracles was to prove that what was happening was from God or whomever God sent in the form of an Old Testament prophet, Messiah, or apostle. It proved that their message was from God.

Once something is established, there is no more reason for certification. Jesus doesn't have to do miracles any longer. The Holy Spirit wrote down the evidence for us to read and believe.

God may have certified Jesus through his miracles, but that only tells us he was approved. The task ahead is to take insight and logic and find faith in Jesus. Paul says, "Faith comes from hearing, and hearing through the word of Christ" (Rom. 10:17).

We know Jesus was approved by God with miracles, but faith will take studying his words. It can't be done any other

Chapter 9 · The Rule of Logic

way. Once we have faith, we can have confidence and hope, for "faith is the assurance of things hoped for, the conviction of things not seen" (Heb. 11:1). Without miracles Jesus is just another wise man. We can put trust in wise men up to a point, but just another wise man can't show us an unseen world. Only one accredited by God can do that.

Logic helps us put clues together to come up with truth. If we handle the Word logically, the Scripture itself will reveal its truth.

What am I saying in all of this? Let me sum it up as simply as I can in this statement. In interpreting any document, including the Bible, we must always strive to find the logical alternative to what we feel is the truth. Our challenge is to extract the most common and simple denominator that makes the most sense. In other words, the truth is the most logical interpretation no matter how complicated it may seem.

> **LOGIC HELPS US PUT CLUES TOGETHER TO COME UP WITH TRUTH.**

Once you eliminate the impossible, what remains, no matter how improbable, must be the truth.

I am quite aware of the difficulty one may face in ferreting out the logic of the Scripture, not to mention mastering the other rules of interpretation. But all of your efforts will pay off.

CHAPTER 10

The Scheme of Redemption

The full narrative of the Bible is God's plan to save man through Christ.

Thus it is written, "The first man Adam became a living being"; the last Adam became a life-giving spirit. But it is not the spiritual that is first but the natural, and then the spiritual. The first man was from the earth, a man of dust; the second man is from heaven. As was the man of dust, so also are those who are of the dust, and as is the man of heaven, so also are those who are of heaven. Just as we have borne the image of the man of dust, we shall also bear the image of the man of heaven. (1 Cor. 15:45–49)

The major narrative of the Bible is that the first man, Adam, was created on earth and is dust, with sin. The last man is Jesus, who was not created but came from heaven and is without sin. Adam sinned and cause a problem God had to solve. Adam lost his position and direct contact with God. Adam could do nothing to restore his position with God; Jesus doesn't need to restore a position, which was never lost. But through him, we may be restored.

It isn't that Jesus was the last man on earth. It's that in the narrative of the Bible, he is the focal point. He is the man the Holy Spirit was waiting to reveal from the beginning, bringing the last man it took to finish the work of our salvation and our redemption.

On the cross Jesus said those mysterious words, "It is finished" (John 19:30). The "Scheme of Redemption" was finished; his work in crushing death had been fulfilled. There is no other man to look to from heaven.

From the Bible's point of view, there is only one objective: to restore to us what we lost through sin—our relationship with God. So the Holy Spirit sees Adam as us—weak and lost—and Jesus as God, a giver of life. The purpose of the "Scheme of Redemption" focuses on the problem created and the problem solved. Everything we read between those two events was God accomplishing that goal.

> THERE IS ONLY ONE OBJECTIVE: TO RESTORE TO US WHAT WE LOST THROUGH SIN.

In the Bible narrative, there are only two men who are important: Adam, whom we see as the first man; and Jesus, the man we needed to fulfill the narrative and restore goodwill between God and man. Therefore, Jesus is that last man: God incarnate.

When the angel appeared to the shepherds, he said, "Glory to God in the highest, and on earth peace among those with whom he is pleased!" (Luke 2:14). He didn't say, "Peace on earth to everyone," as some have misquoted. He said, "Peace among those with whom he is pleased."

There will never be peace on earth, but there is peace in Christ, in his body of believers—his church right now. Is it perfect? No; nothing is perfect this side of heaven. This ability to have peace among those with whom God is pleased was referred to by Paul: "Walk in a manner worthy of the calling to which you have been called, with all humility and gentleness, with patience, bearing with one another in love, eager to maintain the unity of the Spirit in the bond of peace" (Eph. 4:1–3).

Paul was speaking to the church (Christians) at Ephesus, not to the world. He adds the complete commentary on "peace among those with whom he is pleased," declaring that it is among those in the covenant of Christ. Paul lets us know that it takes "humility and gentleness, with patience" to accomplish this. Jesus gave us peace with God, but it is up to us to keep peace among ourselves. He gives us the tools, but we have to make the effort.

We don't often apply many of the scriptures we study to the whole narrative of the Bible. We sometimes pick, choose, and guess at what we feel the Holy Spirit wants to tell us. However, to get the big picture we need a frame, and that frame is the scheme of redemption. Everything needs to stay in that frame.

If we take the position that the Bible is just a collection of books and letters written by those inspired by God, we may come up with the idea that the whole story the Bible presents is a wavering idealism with a particular direction, which at some point provides us with a good way to live, inspired by the man Jesus. But if we look at the whole Bible as the work of the Holy Spirit recording Jesus' mysterious work from creation all the way to his resurrection, we can come away with clearer insight into what the Spirit was presenting.

At the introduction of John's Gospel, he says: "In the beginning was the Word, and the Word was with God, and the Word was God. He was in the beginning with God. All things were made through him, and without him was not anything made that was made" (John 1:1–3).

When we look at Jesus as the beginning and the end result of the Holy Spirit's work, we see a far larger picture than before:

"'I am the Alpha and the Omega,' says the Lord God, 'who is and who was and who is to come, the Almighty'" (Rev. 1:8).

We need to look a little differently at the "Scheme of Redemption" as the total Bible narrative. We need to see Jesus *as* the Bible narrative. We need to see deity as one in all of the Father, Son, and Holy Spirit: the Trinity. But most of all, to understand the Bible narrative we must see Jesus as its focal point; we need to see Jesus as everything.

When the Holy Spirit pens the words, "The revelation of Jesus Christ," at the introduction of the book of Revelation, he is about to fill us in on Jesus' true nature. He's about to tell us that this Jesus is the Alpha and the Omega; the beginning and the end.

What this means is, through Jesus, we have the start (*creation*) continuing to the end (*resurrection*). We have the accomplished nature of God's scheme to save us from sin, which entered into God's creation. We can't blame God, as some do, for our failure causing all of the pain and suffering in the world. You don't get that from the testimony of the Spirit. You get the fact that God created a good place. The Spirit wrote of the creation: "And God saw that it was good" (Gen. 1:25). Then he created man.

Chapter 10 · The Scheme of Redemption

In the beginning, man is the focal point of creation. If man is not the focal point of creation, then why have a creation? If man is the reason for creation, then man needs to have a savior because, having been created a "free moral agent," he will choose wrongly. He must have a choice, or he's not a man but a robot.

After the fall, the Bible narrative turns to bringing Jesus to solve the newly developed problem which will plague mankind for generations: sin. God can't remake the creation; the harm is already done. But he can solve the problem of sin. God can't take soft people out of a hard world, but he can offer victory even in death. God can't force evil people to be good, but he can give his people hope and life.

This is why the whole of Scripture looks forward to one thing: the coming of Christ Jesus.

"To him all the prophets bear witness that everyone who believes in him receives forgiveness of sins through his name" (Acts 10:43).

"Then he said to them, 'These are my words that I spoke to you while I was still with you, that everything written about me in the Law of Moses and the prophets and the Psalms must be fulfilled'" (Luke 24:44).

"Jesus, whom heaven must receive until the time for restoring all the things about which God spoke by the mouth of his holy prophets long ago. Moses said, 'The Lord God will raise up for you a prophet like me from your brothers. You shall listen to him in whatever he tells you. And it shall be that every soul who does not listen to that prophet shall be destroyed from the people.' And all the prophets who have spoken, from Samuel and those who came after him, also proclaimed these days" (Acts 3:20–24).

"But he whom God raised up did not see corruption. Let it be known to you therefore, brothers, that through this man forgiveness of sins is proclaimed to you, and by him everyone who believes is freed from everything from which you could not be freed by the Law of Moses. Beware, therefore, lest what is said in the Prophets should come about: Look, you scoffers,

Be astounded and perish; for I am doing a work in your days, a work that you will not believe, even if one tells it to you" (Acts 13:37–41).

"Peace on earth, good will toward men" doesn't fit the Bible narrative if it doesn't find its fulfillment in Jesus, relative to the people to whom God promised it. He promised it to his covenant people through the blood of Jesus.

Jesus did bring peace on earth and goodwill toward man. The reality is that Jesus brings peace to his people. His people live in peace in his body—the church. Through Jesus' covenant, we have goodwill toward us from God. We sinned and brought judgment upon ourselves. Jesus heals our relationship not only with God but with each other.

"I therefore . . . urge you to walk in a manner worthy of the calling to which you have been called, with all humility and gentleness, with patience, bearing with one another in love, eager to maintain the unity of the Spirit in the bond of peace. There is one body and one Spirit—just as you were called to the one hope that belongs to your call" (Eph. 4:1–4).

That's the Bible narrative: everything is restored in Jesus. Only those who have been called to one hope can produce the bond of peace among themselves through Jesus. Paul was talking to the body of believers in Ephesus. No one in Ephesus outside of Christ was included in Paul's letter.

Chapter 10 · The Scheme of Redemption

The world isn't unified and never will be. "Do not love the world or the things in the world. If anyone loves the world, the love of the Father is not in him. All that is in the world—the lust of the flesh, the lust of the eye and the pride of life—is not from the Father but is from the world" (1 John 2:15–16).

God will not make these people love him. In fact, if they don't turn to be healed, God can't do anything for them as far as the afterlife is concerned. They are free moral agents, and as such, they are entitled to make their own choice. Not everyone is willing to come in and create this peace that finds its fruition in Jesus.

The first prophecy of the Bible is: "I will put enmity between you and the woman, and between your offspring and her offspring; he shall bruise your head, and you shall bruise his heel" (Gen. 3:15). This prophecy sets in motion the redemption narrative of the Bible and its ultimate outcome. Satan will influence his offspring to kill Jesus, but he would rise from that death to crush Satan—a death blow. That's the final outcome.

"These things I have spoken to you, so that in me you may have peace. In the world you have tribulation, but take courage; I have overcome the world" (John 16:33).

The entire Bible revolves around one specific subject: man's relationship with God. The entire Bible is about God's plan for redeeming the fallen back to himself: the Scheme of Redemption.

"If you really want to grow and mature spiritually, then read and study your Bible through the lens of the Scheme of Redemption."

To understand the Scheme of Redemption is to understand the role of the church in the past, the present, and the future. Jesus' work in his body, the church, will affect generations to come.

"Oh, the depth of the riches and wisdom and knowledge of God! How unsearchable are his judgments and how inscrutable his ways! 'For who has known the mind of the Lord, or who has been his counselor?' 'Or who has given a gift to him that he might be repaid?' For from him and through him and to him are all things. To him be glory forever. Amen." (Rom. 11:33–36)

CHAPTER 11

THE COVENANT

God is a covenant God

As Christians, we quote a scripture every Sunday when we observe communion. It's Jesus saying at the Last Supper, "For this is my blood of the covenant, which is poured out for many for the forgiveness of sins" (Matt. 26:28).

We take the juice that represents Jesus' blood, but we don't visit the word "covenant," which he mentions in connection with his blood. This vital statement is to change the relationship of worshipers forever. It is certainly important to the very way we serve God through Jesus.

"This is the covenant that I will make with them after those days, declares the Lord: I will put my laws on their hearts, and write them on their minds" (Heb. 10:16).

In our modern church, we have lost the concept of an Old Testament covenant, replacing it with what we believe to be a contract. A covenant is not the same as a contract. With a covenant, there must be a conquering king, a subjugated people, and ratification by blood. With his new subjects, the king offers a new covenant. This new covenant contains laws and the tribute required of his subjects. The subjects bend to the will of the new king by accepting his offer of a covenant relationship, entering into it and pledging their lives.

Elements of blessings and cursing are read out to the people to accept. There is no alternative. One accepts the terms and receives the blessings they bestow, or they reject the offered covenant, in which case they become enemies of the state and, if caught, receive the cursing (*punishment laid out in the covenant*).

A covenant must be ratified by blood. So to have a covenant, there must be a conquering king, a submissive people, and a covenant sealed by blood. We have a covenant through Jesus; he is our conquering king, and we are his subjects. His new covenant was sealed by his own blood. We can review the terms of the covenant and decide for ourselves if we accept them or not.

> WE HAVE A COVENANT THROUGH JESUS.

We can live in the unity of the spirit in the bond of peace, or we can reject his offer and suffer his wrath. This doesn't mean the king won't have enemies; he will. And we as his people must suffer and deal with those enemies too. But we, as a chosen people, will have peace with each other as citizens of his kingdom.

Every covenant that God makes with humans has the elements of blessings (*promises*) and cursing (*punishment*). Most Christians understand that they agreed to the new covenant with God through the blood of Jesus when they came to Christ. But I don't think most Christians understand the elements of that covenant, which are necessary to obey its particulars. This is why many Christians are suffering in their faith and stumble

CHAPTER 11 · THE COVENANT

in their hope when strange-sounding doctrines are presented to them as truth.

In the book of Ephesians, Paul goes over some of what is expected of the citizens of this kingdom: "Walk in a manner worthy of the calling to which you have been called, with all humility and gentleness, with patience, bearing with one another in love, eager to maintain the unity of the Spirit in the bond of peace. There is one body and one Spirit—just as you were called to the one hope that belongs to your call" (Eph. 4:1–4).

He also mentions his expectations in saying:

> So that we may no longer be children, tossed to and fro by the waves and carried about by every wind of doctrine, by human cunning, by craftiness in deceitful schemes. Rather, speaking the truth in love, we are to grow up in every way into him who is the head, into Christ, from whom the whole body, joined and held together by every joint with which it is equipped, when each part is working properly, makes the body grow so that it builds itself up in love. (Eph. 4:14–16)

God wants stable, productive citizens who benefit the whole and serve at his pleasure. Grow in the knowledge of the law of love. He also tells us what the covenant will not tolerate:

> Now this I say and testify in the Lord, that you must no longer walk as the Gentiles do, in the futility of their minds. They are darkened in their understanding, alienated from the life of God because of the ignorance that is in them, due to their hardness of heart. They have become callous and have given themselves up to sensuality, greedy to practice every kind of impurity. (Eph. 4:17–19)

Some who don't understand the new covenant resort to teachings that are contrary to what Jesus has established. They substitute the facts they don't understand for what they feel is truth or "their truth."

The blood of Jesus is not a magical formula. We should see a conquering king who, for their protection, established laws and demands tribute of those he removed from a kingdom of darkness and placed in a better kingdom.

Paul says, "Giving thanks to the Father, who has qualified you to share in the inheritance of the saints in light. He has delivered us from the domain of darkness and transferred us to the kingdom of his beloved Son, in whom we have redemption, the forgiveness of sins" (Col. 1:12–14).

One of the best passages that explains this concept of a covenant relationship is in Moses's speech as the Israelites are about to enter the Promised Land. He issues them a strong warning concerning the covenant that God made with them at Sinai.

> This day I call to the heavens and the earth as witnesses against you that I have set before you life and death, blessings and curses. Now choose life, so that you and your children may live. (Deut. 30:19)

In the book of Deuteronomy, Moses gives his final words to the Israelites, cautioning them to follow and obey God rather than turning to the false idols. However, later, after the Israelites entered the Promised Land, they left the covenant blessings of God and turned to the idolatry of the people they were displacing.

Our challenges are different choices but the same concept that some turn to in rejecting the new covenant and choosing death over life in Christ.

"Woe to those who call evil good and good evil, who put darkness for light and light for darkness" (Isa. 5:20).

At the Last Supper, Jesus offered up a new covenant that he expects us to submit to if we want to claim the promises and blessings offered. Moses called the Israelites to be deliberate in their actions. Later when the Messiah (Jesus) comes, he speaks in parables, reminding the Jewish people of the same blessings and curses. The parables have one message—do right and be blessed in this life or be cursed in the next, like the parable of the rich man and Lazarus (Luke 16:19–28).

Later, while eating the Passover meal with his disciples, Jesus makes an amazing proclamation. He declares the institution of a new covenant with his soon-to-come new people.

Jesus says, "For this is my blood, which confirms the (new) covenant between God and his people. It is poured out as a sacrifice to forgive the sins of many" (Matt. 26:28, NLT).

The Israelites' choice was to stay pure and dedicated to God. But in time the people of Israel turned away from God's laws and teachings to serve idols. As a result they were scattered throughout the nations. The Babylonian captivity was one of the curses the prophet Jeremiah warned about. The Israelites didn't listen to the warnings to turn back to God and receive the continued blessing of staying in the land, so off to exile they went (a curse).

Still, even as these blessings and curses were being outlined, God foresaw that this would happen and promised that he would bring his people home:

> Even if you have been banished to the most distant land under the heavens, from there the LORD your God will gather you and bring you back. He will bring you to the

> land that belonged to your ancestors, and you will take possession of it. (Deut. 30:4–5)

If they wanted restoration (blessings), they had to repent and turn back to God. There were elements in this covenant they had to uphold. One can return to a covenant relationship with God by turning back to him.

> And when all these things come upon you, the blessing and the curse, which I have set before you, and you call them to mind among all the nations where the Lord your God has driven you, and return to the Lord your God, you and your children, and obey his voice in all that I command you today, with all your heart and with all your soul, then the Lord your God will restore your fortunes and have mercy on you, and he will gather you again from all the peoples where the Lord your God has scattered you." (Deut. 30:1–3)

Along with a stern warning there is, in Jeremiah, a new hope laid out for the future people of God. It would be a new covenant that would be easier to keep—a covenant with new and better blessings.

> Behold, the days are coming, declares the Lord,
> when I will make a new covenant with
> the house of Israel and with the house of Judah.
> It will not be like the covenant
> I made with their fathers,
> when I took them by the hand
> to lead them out of Egypt—
> a covenant they broke,

Chapter 11 · The Covenant

> though I was a husband to them,
> declares the Lord.
> "But this is the covenant I will make with the house of Israel
> after those days, declares the Lord.
> I will put My law in their minds
> and inscribe it on their hearts.
> And I will be their God,
> and they will be My people.
> No longer will each man teach his neighbor or his brother,
> saying, 'Know the Lord,'
> because they will all know Me,
> from the least of them to the greatest, declares the Lord.
> For I will forgive their iniquities,
> and will remember their sins no more. (Jer. 31:31–34)

The covenant made at Sinai after God led Israel from Egypt was a national covenant. A Jewish child was born into this national covenant just because they were born Jewish. They had to be taught about their covenant God. Under the new covenant made by Christ, no one is born as a child into a covenant relationship with God. We must be taught as individuals about God (the gospel); then we are added to the covenant when we repent and turn to God.

The old covenant was a national one between God and Israel. The new covenant in Jesus' blood is made up of individual followers of Christ. The old covenant was inscribed in stone. The new covenant is inscribed on our hearts.

The writer of Hebrews quotes Jeremiah 31:31, applied to the blood of Christ, which confirms this covenant.

> But now Jesus, our High Priest, has been given a ministry that is far superior to the old priesthood, for he is the one who mediates for us a far better covenant with God, based on better promises. If the first covenant had been faultless, there would have been no need for a second covenant to replace it. (Heb. 8:6–7)

The writer of Hebrews explains the failure of the national Jewish covenant made with all Jews and the success of the new covenant, now made with individual Christians.

"When God speaks of a 'new' covenant, it means he has made the first one obsolete. It is now out of date and will soon disappear" (Heb. 8:13).

We can only be under one covenant at a time. We can't be under the old covenant and the new covenant at the same time. There is only one covenant offered to us now. We should be cautious not to bring over elements of the old covenant into the new covenant.

Though the sacrifices of the old covenant were a foreshadowing of Christ's blood, they could not purify those who brought them. "But in these sacrifices there is a reminder of sins every year. For it is impossible for the blood of bulls and goats to take away sins" (Heb. 10:3–4).

"Just think how much more the blood of Christ will purify our consciences from sinful deeds so that we can worship the living God. For by the power of the eternal Spirit, Christ offered himself to God as a perfect sacrifice for our sins" (Heb. 9:14).

"Let us hold tightly without wavering to the hope we affirm, for God can be trusted to keep his promise. Let us think of ways to motivate one another to acts of love and good works. And let us not neglect our meeting together, as some people do, but

Chapter 11 · The Covenant

encourage one another, especially now that the day of his return is drawing near" (Heb. 10:23–25).

The blessings are laid out in the New Testament. However, we must never forget that the curses are there too.

> Dear friends, if we deliberately continue sinning after we have received knowledge of the truth, there is no longer any sacrifice that will cover these sins. There is only the terrible expectation of God's judgment and the raging fire that will consume his enemies. For anyone who refused to obey the Law of Moses was put to death without mercy on the testimony of two or three witnesses. Just think how much worse the punishment will be for those who have trampled on the Son of God, and have treated the *blood of the covenant,* which made us holy, as if it were common and unholy, and have insulted and disdained the Holy Spirit who brings God's mercy to us. For we know the one who said, "I will take revenge. I will pay them back." (Heb. 10:23–30, NLT)

Let's go back to Deuteronomy 30:19 for a look at Moses's statement of "calling on heaven and earth." Moses didn't have the authority in himself to swear as a witness—he appealed to the authority of God by calling on "heaven and earth" as witnesses against the Israelites.

In like manner, heaven and earth show up again but instead as a witness to the promised new blessings in Christ Jesus. "But we are looking forward to the new heavens and new earth he has promised, a (new covenant) world filled with God's righteousness" (2 Pet. 3:13).

Peter talks about the new covenant in its total fulfillment and the old one, which was a curse, having to go.

> But the day of the Lord will come as unexpectedly as a thief. Then the heavens will pass away with a terrible noise, and the very elements themselves will disappear in fire, and the earth and everything on it will be found to deserve judgment. (2 Pet. 3:10)

Peter wasn't talking about the literal earth burning up, just as Moses wasn't talking about the literal "heaven and earth" witnessing, but the curse of the old "heaven and earth" passing away. He was looking forward to the "new heaven and earth" as a blessing— the new covenant and its better promises and blessings in Christ Jesus.

The fulfillment of this was when, as Christ predicted in Matthew 24, the then-standing temple—the last physical vestige of the old covenant—would be torn down. Then the new heavens and the new earth that Peter was looking forward to came. "Then I saw a new heaven and a new earth, for the first heaven and the first earth had passed away, and the sea was no more. And I saw the holy city, New Jerusalem, coming down out of heaven" (Rev. 21:1–2).

The "heavens and earth" spoken of at Sinai and by the writer of the letter to the Hebrews are really the elements of the two covenants. He specifically makes the point that these elements are the covenant promises and that the old covenant promises were shakable. But the new covenant promises are unmovable. God had to shake the old out of its place to institute the new covenant with its better promised blessings. The promises are the blessings.

CHAPTER 11 · THE COVENANT

> Be careful that you do not refuse to listen to the One who is speaking. For if the people of Israel did not escape when they refused to listen to Moses, the earthly messenger, we will certainly not escape if we reject the One who speaks to us from heaven! When God spoke from Mount Sinai his voice shook the earth, but now he makes another promise: "Once again I will shake not only the earth but the heavens also." This means that all of creation will be shaken and removed, so that only unshakable things will remain. (Heb. 12:25–27)

God had to shake the heavens and remove the old covenant to replace it with the new covenant instituted by Jesus. When did this happen? Jesus promised that God would remove the last vestige of the national covenant with Israel, the temple. When it fell, God shook the old covenant out of its place and brought in the unshakable "new heavens and earth." He did this in the year AD 70. And, in proof of this—he did it by the Roman army in the same month and the same day that he destroyed Solomon's temple with the Babylonian army over six hundred years before.

We understand that God used the Assyrians and the Babylonians to punish Israel. But when we get to the Romans destroying the nation of Israel in AD 70, we lose our Bible history. That same lawless nation the Jews used to execute their Messiah, God also used to punish them for rejecting and murdering their Messiah. Jesus illustrated this event in the parable of the tenants. What will the owner of the vineyard do? He will come and destroy the tenants and give the vineyard to others. (Mark 12:1–9). The most reprehensible thing that apostate Jews could have done was kill the son of God. What do you think God was going to do after that? Tear them asunder!

Jerusalem was the Hebrew people's seat of the commonwealth, law, and worship of the covenant that God made through Moses. It is only fitting and completely reasonable that a New Jerusalem would be the figurative representation of the new covenant, which Jesus promised at the Last Supper with his disciples.

> For they could not endure the order that was given, "If even a beast touches the mountain, it shall be stoned." Indeed, so terrifying was the sight that Moses said, "I tremble with fear." But you have come to Mount Zion and to the city of the living God, the heavenly Jerusalem, and to innumerable angels in festal gathering, and to the assembly of the firstborn who are enrolled in heaven, and to God, the judge of all, and to the spirits of the righteous made perfect, and to Jesus, the mediator of a new covenant, and to the sprinkled blood that speaks a better word than the blood of Abel.
>
> See that you do not refuse him who is speaking. For if they did not escape when they refused him who warned them on earth, much less will we escape if we reject him who warns from heaven. At that time his voice shook the earth, but now he has promised, "Yet once more I will shake not only the earth but also the heavens."
>
> Therefore let us be grateful for receiving a kingdom that cannot be shaken, and thus let us offer to God acceptable worship, with reverence and awe, for our God is a consuming fire. (Heb. 12:20–29).

Chapter 11 · The Covenant

This phrase, "yet once more," indicates the removal of things that are shaken—that is, things that have been made—so that the things that cannot be shaken may remain. What cannot be shaken out of its place is the everlasting covenant made in Jesus' blood.

There was a covenant with Adam and Eve before the fall. Let's examine it so we can see that all the covenants had the same attributes.

> And God blessed them. And God said to them, "Be fruitful and multiply and fill the earth and subdue it, and have dominion over the fish of the sea and over the birds of the heavens and over every living thing that moves on the earth." And God said, "Behold, I have given you every plant yielding seed that is on the face of all the earth, and every tree with seed in its fruit. You shall have them for food. And to every beast of the earth and to every bird of the heavens and to everything that creeps on the earth, everything that has the breath of life, I have given every green plant for food." (Gen. 1:30)

Adam and Eve were given great blessings. The only rules were to be fruitful in having children, exercise dominion over practically everything, and not eat of the Tree of the Knowledge of Good and Evil. But when Adam and Eve chose to disobey God, the only thing left for them was the curse of being put out of the Garden and the sufferings they brought on themselves. The covenant relationship between God and Adam and Eve had blessings and curses. The first covenant's laws were "to be fruitful and multiply." The blessings were the Garden, food for the taking, and no toil.

> The Lord God took the man and put him in the Garden of Eden to work it and keep it. And the Lord God commanded the man, saying, "You may surely eat of every tree of the garden, but of the tree of the knowledge of good and evil you shall not eat, for on the day that you heard of it you shall surely die." (Gen. 2:15–17)

God had one rule or law: don't eat the fruit of the Tree of the Knowledge of Good and Evil.

Adam and Eve broke God's law, lost the blessings, and suffered the curses of the covenant. We shouldn't fear Christ's new covenant. We only have to concentrate on loving one another, working to uphold the unity that love produces, and keep ourselves pure. God is faithfully holding us in the new covenant. When he looks at us, he only sees the blood of his son covering us.

An Invitation to Contribute

It is by the grace of God that we even have the opportunity to approach the Bible. Jesus declared when he returned to heaven that he would send the "Spirit of truth" whose work would be to glorify him as God.

"But when the Helper comes, whom I will send to you from the Father, the Spirit of truth, who proceeds from the Father, he will bear witness about me" (John 15:26).

Rules is a book of my understanding, of the Holy Spirit bearing witness to Jesus as God throughout the ages. It's a journey I hope to travel with you. And by "with you," I mean that the next edition should have your thoughts and ideas included.

I am but one man who is trying to understand the Bible and impart what I have learned. My hope is that by working together we can bear witness to Jesus Christ in a more precise way.

I entered this endeavor because, in my own studies, I looked for these rules for help. I read a little blurb in books about rules of interpretation, but those books only mentioned the rules. I searched and searched and could not find a book on these rules. So I worked on one. This is my first effort.

My invitation to you is to contribute your thoughts about these rules. My idea is to brainstorm with you. I have endeavored to explain the rules as best I can. There are some great thinkers out there who see things I may not.

Working together would create a fellowship that would help some who haven't had the chance to write a book but nevertheless have great ideas.

If you send me your thoughts, I will determine if the information will fit comfortably in the book. If that's the case, then I will list you in the credits.

All information forwarded to me shall become my property to do with as I wish. All information and communication you send must be of a positive and helpful nature. Remember, the reason for this book is to glorify Jesus. Do not send any criticism or angry communication if you think the book isn't your cup of tea. It is my cup of tea, and you are invited to make it a better cup of tea.

I have prepared an email address just for this purpose: rulesgenebuckelew@gmail.com.

Thank you for your future help and support.

—Gene Buckelew

Epilogue

I leave you with this food for thought.

Understanding what we read in the Bible is a daunting task for anyone—scholar, theological student, seasoned reader, or a beginner approaching the Scriptures in their initial search for the Bible's truth. *Rules* is just one man's thoughts on the matter of approaching the Bible narrative in a systematic and analytical way.

There are rules in everything we experience in life. There are rules of physics, rules of law—rules, rules, rules. We follow or are affected by them every day. Rules are something we learn from a very early age: We're taught "HOT, do not touch!" "That's enough candy for one day." "No, you can't ride your bike in the street."

We later learn to drive, and somehow along the way, we understand that we will have to follow the "rules of the road." How did we get there? Where along the way did we come to the startling revelation that we must follow rules to accomplish or lawfully be allowed to do anything in life? Was it second nature? Was it engraved into our subconscious in the womb? Was it revealed to us supernaturally?

I don't think any of these things are true. We learned how to reason and understood how to function in life by a set of rules. We used these rules to examine, visualize, and process the world around us. We learned by using "rules of interpretation," not knowing that a set of rules actually existed. We learned how to interpret everything around us by using a set of nine rules. We just never realized there were rules because we learned everything so slowly, over a long period of time, with not a lot of effort.

So why can we read a short story by a contemporary author and understand completely what they are trying to convey? Why can we read articles in our local newspaper and understand "what it's all about"? Well, it's because in our world of experience we know the "rules of interpretation." We grew up with them. We know what a contemporary author means when we read their work. We understand the cultural norms, colloquial ideas, idioms, figures of speech, and context.

We would use the very same rules we unwittingly learned growing up, "interpreting" our surroundings. The very same nine "rules of interpretation" that we use every day without thinking which rule we are using at any given moment. The very same rules that our court system uses to interpret evidence placed before it. The same "rules of interpretation" that the Supreme Court uses to interpret the US Constitution written so long ago.

So why is it that when we approach the Bible, we lose all touch with these "rules of interpretation," which are so easy to apply in our everyday lives? We lose our skill of deduction and can become so confused that we come up with convoluted nonsense. We resort to ideas like, "The Bible means something different to each person." Or, "The Holy Spirit talks to me, and that's how I know what the Bible means."

I believe it is because we have never formally been taught these rules. Maybe, if you attended law school or majored in history, you were familiarized with them. However, the average person wouldn't be able to quote one single rule of these nine, let alone consciously tell someone how to apply them. However, I believe that if we diligently learn these rules and honestly apply them, we can come closer to understanding what we read from the Bible.

About the Author

GENE BUCKELEW has studied and taught the Bible for over fifty years. Having earned a Bachelor's in Biblical Studies from Sunset International Bible Institute, he's passionate about teaching Bible truths in a way that produces an investigative student. He and his wife, Tracy, live in Tyngsborough, Massachusetts.